Viral Personal Branding

Mike Allebach

Copyright © 2019 by Michael Allebach

All rights reserved. This book or any portion thereof
may not be reproduced or used in any manner whatsoever without the
express written permission of the publisher except for the use of brief
quotations in a book review.

ISBN - 9781794297548

405 East Walnut Street
North Wales, Pa 19454

This book is dedicated to my family who has been patient during the writing of this book Rachel, Elijah, Evan and Caleb and to the people who have mentored, inspired and believed in me: Walter Sawatzky, Steve Saporito, Jason Groupp, Jaleel King, Andrew Funderburg, Jonathan Min-Wook Main, Hillary Yasmer Shemin, Kristen Kidd and Lee Shelly.

Contents

Viral Personal Branding	7
Who You Are: Your Personal Brand Recipe	19
Who You Serve	33
Branding, Marketing and Finding Your Niche	41
Designing Your Net: Finding and Catching Clients	51
Creating Viral Content	99
Creating a Tribe: A Community of Belonging	113
Case Studies	123

Introduction

Viral Personal Branding

The train dropped me off in Midtown Manhattan on a crisp, fall afternoon a decade ago. I trekked 12 blocks through the hustle and bustle to a secret event. Serendipitously, I had scored a golden ticket to see Seth Godin, one of the biggest thought leaders in the marketing space. Along with 30 other winners, I'd see his virgin presentation on his New York Times Bestseller, *Tribes*.

On the surface level, I knew what creating a tribe was about. Seth had taught the importance of creating a remarkable business and niche, or, as he called it, a "purple cow." He was one of the most prominent personal brands out there. He marketed himself and his career as a brand. The pure definition of personal branding.

Then Seth gave his presentation, one of the best I'd ever witnessed. He spoke about working on projects you believe in and surrounding yourself with people who believe in your mission. I was on board with every word he uttered.

What I didn't know was that Seth would ask us to critique

his performance and presentation after it was over. He was one of the most prominent minds in business and marketing. Why was he asking us? I thought Seth was the expert.

Too nervous to raise my hand to critique him, I snapped a quick photo of him on the sly. I snuck out without talking to anyone.

The next day, I emailed the photo to Seth with a little thank you note. To my surprise, Seth wrote back and gave me a compliment on a great picture. The interaction was so meaningful, I printed the email out and posted it to the wall. In a world where I felt invisible and lost, suddenly I felt seen. That short little email was posted to my wall for the following five years. My hero had noticed. He flipped my thanks into making it about me. Great personal brands always bring back the focus to their tribe and the community they lead. In Seth's words, "If you show up regularly with generosity, everything else is gonna take care of itself."

This is the paradox. The best personal brands do meaningful work and give purpose to others. They create belonging, community, and understanding.

So what exactly is going viral?
Brands and ideas can become contagious. Going viral is spreading a message or idea quickly to a large group of people. Just like the common cold, your message and ideas can spread the same way. We'll explore how to be

remarkable and why some stories spread. This book lists ingredients to viral content and triggers the active our brain to share stories. Viral is in essence word-of-mouth accelerator.

We will look at how your personal journey relates to your business. This is the very foundation of both going viral and your personal brand. You will first need to clarify your own beliefs and your message in order to build a community.

Maybe at first glance, this appears narcissistic. This is the paradox I was talking about. The change first starts inside you. As you grow and share your story, it changes and attracts others. We'll explore the intersection of perception others have of you and the perception you have about yourself. After you set your foundation, your success on this journey depends on how you treat others. It's about them. People who need to get what you have and need a guide for their dreams. You have an idea of how to make your community a bit better and, in turn, make the world a bit better.

This book is about what happened in the decade following Seth Godin's "Tribes" presentation. It covers what I learned along my way. How I learned to create viral content, attract dream clients, and build tribes of my own.

By the end of this book, you'll know five things about your personal brand:
1. Who you are

2. What you do
3. Who you serve
4. What your clients need
5. The magic result your clients get from what you offer

You'll understand how to stand out, stand up for what you believe, how blending in is hurting you, and how you can be unleashed. The most successful marketers and brands understand people at the deepest level. We are illuminating a path for them to follow their dreams and overcome challenges.

The temptation will be to skip the foundation. Don't fall for this trap. Without your foundation, you won't have the personal branding power you need to spread stories within your industry.

This book is written from the trenches just for you. By picking up this book, I know you want to take your venture to the next level. Whether you are an entrepreneur, a band looking for a big break, realtor to the stars, or chiropractor, this was written for you. It's time to level up. Getting noticed, getting press, and getting your dream clients are within your reach. You'll learn how to build your personal brand foundation, be remarkable, get press with a killer hook, and get more clients than ever before. These are the hacks branding and press relations professionals know but don't share. All the tools to get to the next level are in here. This is a book about breaking through your personal limitations while being a practical guide for those who want to go viral, get on TV, in magazines, get famous, or find their ideal clients.

Once you have your foundation of who you are and what you do, you'll be able to move onto making shit happen.

As Zig Ziglar famously put it, "You can get everything in life you want if you will just help enough other people get what they want."

Emotionally, people want three things: to be seen, heard, and loved. I felt these things when Seth Godin wrote back with a compliment of my skill.

In the wise words of Maya Angelou, "I've learned that people will forget what you said, people will forget what you did, but people will never forget how you made them feel."

Once we have our base of who we are and what we do, we are free to serve the world. It's easy to feel a little lost, invisible, or misunderstood.

This is a spark, a start to a new way of being. My hope is you'll unleash the badassery you have bottled up inside. First, we'll have to change the way we see ourselves to help others understand us better. The personal side of branding begins when we work to shed the layers of self-doubt.

Picking up this book is the start of a new chapter in your life.

This is your mountain to climb. You have your big idea. Your peak is ahead. Just like all great novels, a protagonist had a dream and was willing to overcome conflict.

Although you'll have to do the inner work, it's not about you. It never has been. Your personal brand is not about creating something for yourself. Very few people will care about that. It's about creating something that inspires people to have a better life and ultimately giving them more meaning. This is the paradox of personal branding.

Advertising is the Tax for Not Getting Press
"Dude, I can't keep up. I've been responding all weekend, but they are coming in faster than I can answer them."

I was still waking up and slightly confused, "What do you mean? How many people did you get today?"

"Hundred or so."

"You mean a hundred in total, right?" I said

"No, I mean a hundred or two hundred a day since we last spoke. I can't keep up, my email is blowing up."

I went silent for a bit. "Let's get you in and formulate a plan on how to handle all of these leads."

That was the conversation I had one morning after we launched a campaign two months earlier. A local artist came to me with an idea I thought was viral enough to spread his artistic vision worldwide without spending any money on marketing or advertising. This was the testing grounds for building a brand faster than I had ever attempted before. People wanted the artistic service he offered. It was unique, so I put together a marketing launch plan to make him go viral.

I started by filming a video, taking photos, and reaching out to my contacts in the media. Custom pitches were crafted for each media outlet I pursued. I'd had a string of mini-viral successes in the past, but this was crazy. Soon enough, Huffington Post and AOL picked up the video and made a shorter version of it, and we watched the counter go from one million to two million and then all the way up to 11 million views. Even my Facebook friends were non-stop sharing this video, and it was all over my social media feeds. It was bananas!

Each client he booked was worth between $1,000 and $3,000. Getting a 100 leads a day, you can do the math. He was sitting on a goldmine of viral success.

Going Viral: How Ideas and Stories Spread
You might be asking how can I spread my message so the right people find me and pay me what I'm worth? You have a fantastic idea or make amazing art or can solve a human problem. You know you have something worthwhile, but you lack the right number of people who will pay you what you deserve. Let's solve this problem.

At its core, viral is the way stories spread. It latches onto the human phenomenon of word-of-mouth and to the power of the press. Much like a virus spreads person to person, ideas and stories can spread person to person. Viral Branding is the process of taking the friction out of sharing what you do. My goal is to give you the tools to easily share your story and message. In turn, your clients, fans, and friends will spread your message. We'll investigate what makes messages "viral." What makes people want to talk about ideas and share them? We'll explore the social currency your friends, journalists, and evangelists get from spreading your message.

It's been said that advertising is the tax you pay for not getting press. The more word-of-mouth and free press you get, the more your videos and business get shared online for free, the more profit that stays in your pocket.

The Return on Investment of Viral
People ask the ROI on viral. I point to my business. I would not still be a photography entrepreneur if I hadn't learned marketing and sales. My business, start to finish, is based on the strategies in this book. More than half of my bookings and profit for three years were directly tied to a few viral articles I had written. One of those articles alone was shared by 37,100 people and read by hundreds of thousands more. Using these techniques, I've made my brand easy to talk about. Features for TV and radio have come from applying the principles in this book. I have pitched to and been covered by Cosmopolitan, Daily Mail UK, National Examiner, Philadelphia Inquirer, Huffington Post, Petapixel, Fstoppers, Buzzfeed, Inked Magazine, and

Rebel Ink Magazine just to name a few.

The end result of following what's written here is getting your dream clients. People who will respect your work and pay more money, so you can get off the spinning hamster wheel. When you book or sell to someone, you'll say, "These are my people! They get me." It's the no bullshit, no-filler guide to crafting that viral brand. My hope is you'll wake up every Monday stoked to work on your business.

Over 10 years ago, I crafted a niche for myself. First, as the Tattooed Bride Photographer and, more recently, as the Couples Boudoir Photographer Guy.

This takes persistence, drive, and passion. You'll see actual screenshots of messages and emails. While many books tell you how, mine will show you the actual emails I sent. Sometimes, what you'll see is so simple you'll wonder if I'm making it up. I assure you it is. It's time to be remarkable.

Imposter Syndrome
A little note about imposter syndrome. I want to let you in on a little secret I've learned: Every artist and entrepreneur I know gets scared. We question ourselves. At some point in the process of creating things worthwhile, you will face fear.

You might be asking who am I to bring my ideas to the world? Who am I to get up on stage? Why should I get this privilege when I know I'm not the best in my field? What if they find out I'm not the best? What if they find out I'm not even that good? What if people find out I don't really know what I'm doing?

These are the questions from the person Amanda Palmer calls the Fraud Police in her AFP Commencement speech. They are thoughts we all may find as we take this journey toward a viral personal brand.

Let me make this perfectly clear, you do not have to go to business school or art school. No one will give you permission to follow this path. So I'm giving you permission. The next time the band Imposter Syndrome and the Fraud Police show up to play in your head, boo them off the stage. Tell them their song sucks, and you don't want to sing along anymore. The world needs your best. We need your message.

Sometimes we go through dry spells. Sometimes we don't feel one ounce of creativity. Being famous won't make this easier. When you get to do what you really, really love and get recognized for it, the more of a fraud you think you are. You'll probably wonder if your success is a fluke. Maybe you'll even convince yourself you don't deserve this notoriety.

Recognize this is the curse of creating a personal brand. You may have to battle the idea of unworthiness. Just know almost every artist and entrepreneur before you fought this.

Chapter 1

"If you find yourself asking yourself and your friends, 'Am I really a writer? Am I really an artist?' chances are you are. The counterfeit innovator is wildly self-confident. The real one is scared to death."
- Steven Pressfield, The War of Art

Who You Are: Your Personal Brand Recipe

What is a personal brand? In its purest form, a personal brand is an intersection of how people perceive you and how you perceive yourself. This perception happens on three levels.

Auditory: Your Message
Visually: Your Look
Kinesthetically: How You Make People Feel

Uniquely using your values in these three interactions will be your foundational personal brand recipe. So let's build a personal brand that makes your ideal client's mouth water.

Almost a decade ago, I was a full-time marketing and communications director of a non-profit. On the side, I was moonlighting as a wedding photographer, doing rather well for a side hustle. That train soon got derailed. On May 29, my twin boys were born at 30 weeks via emergency c-section. They spent the next month in the NICU at a hospital an hour away from my home.

The experience of having two children in the NICU an hour away wrecked me emotionally. The lack of sleep and emotional state led to my boss forcing me to take some of the summer off. They saw I was emotionally gone and tired. I couldn't find an ounce of focus. I sought medical help in therapists, modern medicine, and eventually met a guru named Walter Sawatzky. He is a soft-spoken man, who knew how to ask the right questions at the right time. He helped me discover my focus again. This built my personal brand foundation.

Some of the exercises in the following pages are ones my guru Walter gave to me. They brought clarity to me when I had none. If you don't have a clear sense of who you are, they will help you find, define, and redefine yourself. Before you share your message, it will need to be clarified.

While philosophers would love to debate the reason for human existence ad nauseam, I'm going to skip it, and say your purpose for being here is the one you assign yourself. You can go big or you can stay small. It's none of my business what you define as your purpose and really nobody else's. All that matters is that you start looking at what you can provide to the world and discover something so meaningful, it will help you work through the tedious and tough days.

If I had to narrow my own existence down to one word, I'd say "empowerment." As a photographer, I strive to have every family, every couple, and every person who walks through the doors leave better than they came in.

In addition to my core value of empowerment, Walter the Guru helped me discover my five supporting values: creating spaces of acceptance, discovery, bringing comfort, believing that everyone is a rockstar inside.

Let's be honest, people aren't very good at talking about themselves or thinking about their own remarkability. It either comes off as braggadocious or self-deprecating. So taking a look at ourselves to help craft our person brand recipe, we'll need to use written exercises. Very few people can talk about their talents.

To understand personal branding, we have to explore human psychology a bit. The personal brands we idolize are what Abraham Maslow, the American Psychologist, refers to as "self-actualized" and "self-transcendent."

Flashing back to high school, you might remember Maslow's hierarchy of needs typically shown as a pyramid.

At the first level of the pyramid are physiological needs including water, food, sleep, clothing, shelter, and sex. The second level is safety. The third level is social and community needs such as friendship, intimacy, and belonging. The fourth level is esteem, which is ego driven.

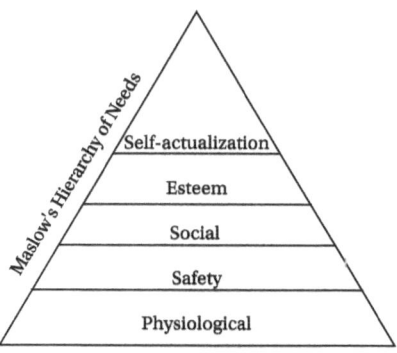

The final two levels at the top of the pyramid are self-actualization and self-transcendent, the understanding of yourself and working toward your own betterment. Self-transcendence is the ability to work toward the betterment of humankind. For many entrepreneurs, this is the goal. Congratulations, if you've picked up this book. You are somewhere in your journey of self-actualization or self-transcendence.

According to Maslow, self-actualized people have many of these characteristics:
- Truth
- Goodness
- Beauty
- Wholeness
- Aliveness
- Uniqueness
- Completion
- Justice
- Order
- Simplicity
- Richness

- Effortlessness
- Playfulness
- Self-sufficiency and autonomy

People who are self-actualized are magnetic to their friends and clients. Sometimes they are polarizing as well, as they attract people with a cult-like status, and push others away like the opposite side of a magnet.

As you may remember, a personal brand is an intersection of how others see us and how we perceive ourselves. So we'll first look through the lens of other people.

The first exercise to discover your foundation came from Walter, my coach. He had me reach out to five of my friends and ask them the top three good things that exist when I'm present and what is missing when I'm missing. This exercise is so powerful that I contact photography client's friends sometimes (with their permission, of course) to find out what their friends love the most about them.

At the time, I was struggling with low-grade social anxiety and stage fright. To a degree, I still feel awkward in large social settings. The feedback I got was life changing. Nobody mentioned I was shy. All the ideas I had about myself were wrong. The story I told myself was a lie. This is one of the most significant hurdles for personal branding. Let's work on rewriting this story.

Exercise 1
Ask five friends these questions:
What happens when I show up?
What happens when I'm not there?

Let your friends know that you are going through personal branding exercise when you ask them to complete this exercise. This way, it doesn't seem like you're fishing for compliments. If everyone participates, you'll have 10 other ideas of who you are.

Look for things that are duplicated at least once between the answers. Circle all of those things that will help you to develop your five values. We are looking at the most essential part of personal branding, defining ourselves and what we stand for. This is the beginning of living out your own brand. If you were a corporation, these would formulate your mission and values.

Some of your friend's answers should be of no surprise. If you are like me, you'll get a little feedback on things that were a bit unexpected.

Exercise 2
Who are the five people in the world you most look up to? Write their names down on the next page.

Now, write down the unique things you admire about each person.

Now, read the list of what you admire the most about

them, but put "I am" in front of each thing you admire.

This list represents the values you see in yourself as wanting to develop. Your core values.

Narrow it down from 15 words and ideas down to your top five. Then narrow these words and ideas down to your number one. This is your personal word. Oddly enough, your word doesn't ever need to appear on your website or anywhere else. Once you know what your word is, you can start to live out your personal brand. My personal word is "empower." What I do as a couples boudoir photographer is empowering. Photography is my method and tool. This word is literally branded in a tattoo on my arm. You don't have to go that far in personal branding yourself, but, hey, if you find your word, don't be afraid to get it tattooed on your body.

Supporting values are your other words. These are things that you can talk about when you're thinking of content for your website or blog. These are great ideas for your videos or anything that you're doing to support your personal brand.

When I go to networking events, my favorite question to ask is "What is your story?" This question always gets a little laugh, awkward silence, and then people smile and tell you their story.

So my question for you is what is your back story? It's like Spiderman and Superman. Everyone has a back story.

You have a back story, too. How did you get to this very moment? It's what brought you to this point today. It might be significant, or it might feel insignificant to you. Don't discount this. It's an essential piece to building your personal brand values. If you could point to one moment as the defining moment that brought you to the place that you are today and has you doing what you love to do, what would that moment be? A couple questions you could ask yourself would be:

What is the moment of biggest pain in my life?
What was my moment of clarity?
What was the moment when I knew that this is what I was called to do?

Toyota and the Seven Levels of Your Why
Simon Sinek made the "why" of what you are doing legendary with his 2009 TED talk (https://www.ted.com/talks/simon_sinek_how_great_leaders_inspire_action). In 17 minutes, he talked about how the best businesses inspire by knowing their "why." Knowing why they do what they do is the key to their success. Prior to Simon Sinek's video, Toyota made their business thrive on getting to the root of issues with the "why" question. Why did things fail and why did problems happen?

Through asking why seven times, they were able to discover the root of the problem. This led them to being one of the most reliable car manufacturers.

Taiichi Ohno, Former Executive Vice President of Toyota

Motor Corporation, explains it this way:

"We come across problems in all sorts of situations in life, but, according to Taiichi Ohno, pioneer of the Toyota Production System in the 1950s, "Having no problems is the biggest problem of all." Ohno saw a problem not as a negative, but, in fact, as "a kaizen (continuous improvement) opportunity in disguise." Whenever one cropped up, he encouraged his staff to explore problems first-hand until the root causes were found. "Observe the production floor without preconceptions," he would advise. "Ask 'why' five times about every matter."
He used the example of a welding robot stopping in the middle of its operation to demonstrate the usefulness of his method, finally arriving at the root cause of the problem through persistent inquiry:

1. **"Why did the robot stop?"** The circuit has overloaded, causing a fuse to blow.
2. **"Why is the circuit overloaded?"** There was insufficient lubrication on the bearings, so they locked up.
3. **"Why was there insufficient lubrication on the bearings?"** The oil pump on the robot is not circulating sufficient oil.
4. **"Why is the pump not circulating sufficient oil?"** The pump intake is clogged with metal shavings.
5. **"Why is the intake clogged with metal shavings?"** Because there is no filter on the pump.

Even if initially time-consuming, identifying the root cause of a problem is important, because it allows us to take appropriate countermeasures to prevent recurrence in the long-term. "The root cause of any problem is the key to a lasting solution," Ohno used to say. He constantly emphasized the importance of genchi genbutsu, or going to the source, and clarifying the problem with one's own eyes. "Data is, of course, important in manufacturing," he often remarked, "but I place greatest emphasis on facts."

Our last exercise is the seven levels to discovering your why! Each level will bring you a deeper understanding into your purpose.

1. Why did you pick up this book?

2. Why is that important?

3. Why is that important to you?

4. Why did you focus on this?

5. Why does that matter?

6. Why does that matter?

7. Why do you say that?

Your seventh level "why" is the core of why you do what you do! Or, at least, why you picked up the book. Just as Toyota uses this to discover problems, you can use this as the compass for your life along with your values, mission, and message.

Standing Up to Stand Out

Corporate brands have beliefs and values guiding their business, so can personal brands. And, let's be honest, many corporations aren't very good at sticking to their stated values and beliefs. You can do better. Use your values to guide your content creation strategy for your website and social media. To stand out, you will need to stand up for what you believe in. Put the weight behind your values. If you think your services should be affordable to the masses, then price accordingly. If you believe that you offer a luxury, then make people save up for you. If you believe in LGBTQ inclusivity, make sure your future clients know (this is one of my personal brand's values). Your values have a cost. They will push some people away and push other people toward you.

Share articles and videos made by others who share the same values and beliefs. Being vanilla is boring. Stand out by standing up. Be a little polarizing with your message while providing the best service you can. Not everyone will love what you do and that's fine. You aren't Walmart, you don't need to please everyone. It's simply impossible.

Boring doesn't cut through to the attention of consumers anymore. As you craft your message and your pitch and your personal brand, you'll find your uniqueness. You can stand out if you give yourself permission. Maybe you've been afraid to show the unboring parts of your personal brand.

Where could you be bolder? For you, this book might be a sign to let your freak flag fly. Step outside your comfort zone. Don't water yourself down. The number-one reason people don't have a viral personal brand is they haven't given themselves permission to change their narrative. Their story is written timidly. Stepping back in time, I see this was the story I told myself. I believed I couldn't make a difference, nobody cared, nobody liked my ideas. When I rewrote my story, it became "I create spaces for people to belong and create change in small communities. I empower people with the gifts they possess."

What You Do
Your story, your values, and your mission have brought you to this very point. Own what you are qualified to do. You believe in the possibility of a better community that's why you've picked up this book. The story we told ourselves has served us until this point. If we want to dream bigger and do bigger things, we need to realize our potential.

Our vision for a brighter future for others starts with a vision for ourselves. If we don't believe we have something to offer, we won't offer it. Learning about the gifts we possess helps others find their greatness. When we view our story in the context of community and our clients, we discover a great power. The story we tell ourselves shifts the story we tell others. Greatness and transformation are contagious.

Marianne Williamson beautifully illustrates this

phenomenon:

"Our deepest fear is not that we are inadequate. Our deepest fear is that we are powerful beyond measure. It is our light, not our darkness that most frightens us. We ask ourselves, Who am I to be brilliant, gorgeous, talented, and fabulous? Actually, who are you not to be? You are a child of God. Your playing small does not serve the world. There is nothing enlightened about shrinking so that other people will not feel insecure around you. We are all meant to shine as children do. We were born to make manifest the glory of God that is within us. It is not just in some of us; it is in everyone and as we let our own light shine, we unconsciously give others permission to do the same. As we are liberated from our own fear, our presence automatically liberates others."

Chapter 2

Who You Serve

Every year, my studio has a booth at the largest tattoo convention in the United States. We sell sessions to our studio and advertise tattooed weddings. This past year a couple walked by our booth holding hands and I could feel they were my kind of clients.

I yelled to them, "Have you ever had photos taken together?"

They yelled back "We're not good-looking enough for photos."

"Bullshit! That's a lie! Get your asses over here and check out these photos." I told them.

I proceeded to ask them questions and their response was, "How are you reading our minds?"

It wasn't magic, I know the type of people my photography appeals to. We were at a tattoo show, not a bridal show so cursing and jokingly yelling at passers by was appropriate. My gut told me to fight for them. With a few quick questions I know what type of client they potentially are, and I'm able to speak directly to those people with precision. They were holding hands so most likely in a new relationship. Communication was open and honest, which means they've most likely gone through a string of bad relationships before. Talking to hundreds of couples in a year allows me to quickly assess if a client matches any of our client avatars.

They came into the studio, their photos turned out amazing, and they thanked me for being persistent at the tattoo convention. The photos we made together helped them level up their relationship and gave them something tangible to look at every day in their home.

This is the magic of knowing who you serve. When you talk to each future client in their language, they respond like you are a mind reader to them. They feel understood and become open to buying.

Create meaning for people so your ideal clients will magnetically be attracted to you. Get clients what they want. Most people start the opposite way around. They create things they want to sell. This is the wrong way to go at it. Your clients have unaddressed needs and wants.

To create meaning for your clients, you need to deeply understand your clients. Viral personal brand leaders understand this is about helping your clients get what they want in life. People want to be seen, heard, and loved. They care about their health, money, and relationships. If you can help them to be seen her loved, or help them in health, money, and relationships, you will have a great career. What do your future clients want in their lives?

These are the nine questions that are going to help you with who you serve:
1. What is being overlooked by others in my industry?
2. What are my clients' fears?
3. What are my clients' dreams?
4. What do my clients want and need?
5. How are they going to change as a result?
6. What happens if they fail to make a change?
7. What do they currently believe?
8. Why do clients come to you?
9. Why didn't the clients come to you?

The first niche clients I served were tattooed brides. I had this crazy idea one day to put a tattooed model in a wedding dress. Back in 2007, nobody was posting photos of tattooed brides. My hope was one day it would be acceptable for a bride have tattoos in a wedding dress. This crazy idea became reality the next year when I first photographed my first tattooed bride in a wedding dress. At that moment, I was afraid to put it on my website. My gut said to do it anyway, and I made it the first photo on my website. I thought the photo would scare mothers' of the bride off, but ultimately I believed in my idea.

One of my first brides after the photo was posted said she had paid and signed a contract with another photographer. Then in a later conversation, he told her he would photoshop out her tattoos. She said, "I paid a lot of good money for these tattoos, and I'm not having you photoshop them out."

Fulfilling our clients' secret desires is one of the best ways to serve them. As we look to position ourselves in the marketplace and find our niche, one of the best ways to do this is look for areas that are under-represented and overlooked.

Where are clients being missed? What is something I can do, something no one else can? What is my industry blind to at the moment? Go back and fill in your answers.

One of my supporting values is acceptance. In my example of tattooed brides, their dream is to have a beautiful, meaningful wedding without being judged. Being judged is one of their biggest fears.

What Do Your Clients Need?
Your clients hold beliefs that keep them from their goals. They also have unmet needs and wants. Spend time talking with your clients to uncover the products or services you can offer to fulfill these needs and wants.

My dream clients have a lot of things in common. Not only do they have tattoos, but they also put a high value on acceptance and their relationships. Later on, we will talk about sharing things not only what you've written but also what other people have written, or videos that relate to your clients. This is a great way to engage with your clients.

The Magic Result Your Clients Get From What You Offer
It has been said people don't buy a drill; they buy the hole that it creates. They don't buy the hole it creates either. They buy it to build the treehouse for their child or repair their grandmother's antique chair.

You can discover the magic result your current clients get easily. Take all of your thank-you notes and reviews and then put the words into a word cloud program like Wordle.com .

This exercise might take you an hour or so because you'll have to remove words like "if," "the," and prepositions and common nouns. What you'll get as a result from this exercise is the thing they're telling their friends about. This is the gift, the magic result you've given to them.
Feel free to dive in deep by interviewing your favorite clients and ask them how they changed as a result of working with you.

Digging deeper is something we don't always like to think about doing. What happens when somebody books a competitor or fails to book you at all? What result in their life will they miss? How much longer will it take them to achieve what they want to achieve? Or what could happen to them that is bad?

In my case of tattooed brides, they could get a photographer who isn't accepting of tattoos. The photographer could even make fun of them.

It's good to find out how your clients found you, but more importantly, why they booked you. What was that one thing that made the difference? Why exactly did they book you?

Interview five clients that you love. Ask them why they booked you.

In the beginning, many artists, service providers, and entrepreneurs get booked based on price. That rarely lasts for long as the realities of work and profit set in. If your clients are initially telling you price is the reason why they booked, go a little further. Find out more. "Well, why did you book me even though there were other affordable people doing the same thing that I do?"

Appeal to your ideal clients emotionally.

Finally, if you're able to ask people why they didn't book, you may find some really good gems. Sometimes, they are things that you shouldn't fix. If you have targeted a demographic that is serving you well, don't worry much that another demographic isn't picking you. Some things you should fix, though. It isn't serving your personal brand to ignore emails or phone calls. Obviously, if you come across this information, you'll want to use it to fix your process for finding and booking clients.

Oh and one last hack I found right before this book went to press: Facebook Audience Insights! Google the link for this one. You can find out every bit of information about people who follow your Facebook Page you could ever imagine. This is a goldmine of info! To get started, head to facebook.com/ads/audience_insights

My audience info for Couples Boudoir Photo Guy on Facebook

(New Audience)
6.6K monthly active people

People on Facebook
Country: United States of America

| Demographics | Page Likes | Location | Activity |

Top Categories

#	Category	Example
1	Photographer	Allebach Photography
2	Games/Toys	Lisa Frank
3	Women's Clothing Store	The Violet Vixen · Yandy.com · Debshops
4	Gas Station	Sheetz
5	Social Club	Lost Pinup
6	Website	WeddingWire · Weird Nature · Unspeakable Crimes · Mom's Got Ink
7	Publisher	Petty Mayonnaise
8	TV Show	31 Nights of Halloween
9	Interest	Tattoo acceptance in the workplace
10	Apparel & Clothing	Chubby Girls

See All

Page Likes
Facebook Pages that are likely to be relevant to your audience based on Facebook Page likes.

Page	Relevance	Audience	Facebook	Affinity
Allebach Photography	1	820	24.2K	10312x
The Violet Vixen	2	853	662.7K	391x
Bad Kitty USA	3	843	947.5K	270x
WeddingWire	4	898	1.1m	259x
Lisa Frank	5	780	921.5K	257x
Yandy.com	6	1.1K	1.4m	243x
Weird Nature	7	775	1m	233x
Magic Men	8	915	1.3m	220x
Unspeakable Crimes	9	1.1K	1.5m	218x

Chapter 3

Branding, Marketing and Finding Your Niche

My hope is you'll find your own little niche in the world and get your dream clients from it. And a bonus of this is the tighter your niche, the easier it is to get free press from it.

I've heard it said; "It's better to be a big fish in a small pond rather than being a small fish in a big pond." This is what I found to be true in my own business. I've worked in two niches over the last 10 years: photographing tattooed weddings and couples' boudoir.

As you work on finding your niche, know that you can only build one niche at a time. In my experience, it takes roughly two years to be known as the to-go expert in your field locally. You might be able to have much quicker results if you already have a following, and you are already considered an expert. I'm not going to sugarcoat it. This takes work and hustle. Don't worry. I'm going to guide you through the whole process of becoming the niche expert.

Let's say you're a makeup artist. Finding a niche would be getting more specific than just a generalized makeup artist. Now, I know what you're thinking. If I have a niche,

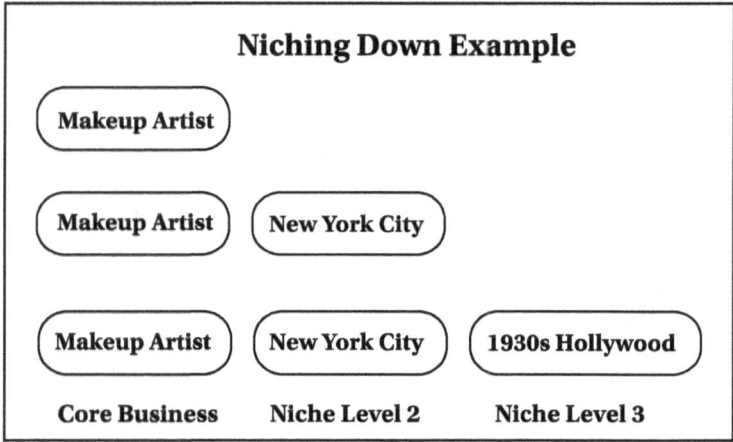

isn't that going to prevent me from booking outside of the niche? That's not my experience. I still get pet photography requests and book them even though I don't have them listed on my website. When you are seen as an expert in one area, people will latch onto you. They will say, "I know you do this and this, but could you do X Y and Z for me?"

Okay, so back to the makeup artist. If you want to go one level deep, you can choose a location or a specialty. What this would look like is, let's say, the makeup artist specialized in the 1930s' Hollywood Glamour look-alike hair and makeup. That's that's one level deep. Two levels deep would be 1930s hair in New York City. If using a location to go two levels deep in your niche, make sure your metro area has a minimum of 100,000 people.

So you could be the number-one expert in your Rhode Island area in whatever you do, or you could be your number one in Providence. Higher population areas like Manhattan, Los Angeles, and Phoenix may want to consider going three levels deep in your niche.

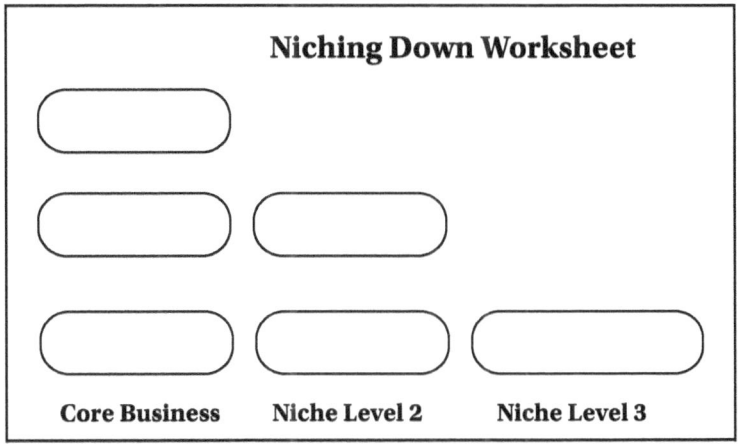

Nickname to Fame

If you are on Instagram or LinkedIn, I highly recommend finding your nickname. This doesn't have to appear anywhere on the web other than Facebook, Instagram, or LinkedIn. You can include it on your website if applicable. I find that on both Facebook and Instagram nicknames are a great way to connect with people. I remember a marketing guru who went by the "nametag guy." He would wear a nametag on his jacket, then underneath on his t-shirt, and then, underneath that, he had his nametag tattooed on his chest. This is commitment. Something as silly as this nickname and his nametag got him international speaking gigs. Sometimes the most ridiculous things are the most powerful.

Each of my niches have their own Instagram with their own nickname. Realtors in urban areas are using this tactic, and they put their nickname on the sign. Depending on your area of expertise, this may or may not work. One of the best ways it can work in your favor is by having a press release that includes your nickname. When you submit your press release to the newspaper, the media will pick up on your nickname. They will call you by it, and then you can reference that in your advertising. How genius is that marketing? Your nickname should be short and maybe even funny.

Creating Your Tagline
Next is your tagline. I view a tagline as the general pitch for your business. We'll be talking about crafting pitches later. Trust me, your tagline is going to take you a while to craft. A tagline should be a short sentence of either your values or how your clients change as a result of what you do.

With my personal word being "empower," I wanted a tagline conveying this idea. So my tagline is "Connect to Your Badass." This tagline works as an umbrella over my branding headshot business, tattooed wedding photography, and over my couples' boudoir work. Couples connect to the badass that lives inside of each other and inside of themselves. It took me two months to craft this tagline, so if you can't think of one right away, don't be worried.

Your tagline creation process is a great way to bring along

clients into the brainstorming process. If you have a Facebook group for your clients, this is a wonderful place to have them involved. They'll be able to help you see what works and what doesn't. When I brought this idea up, they mentioned the word "badass" or "badassery." So I made sure that this word made it into the final tagline. Along the way, there were approximately 25 different variations. My recommendation is to brainstorm at least 25 ideas for your tagline. Do testing with your clients and see how they react to your tagline; if it doesn't resonate, you can't use it. You can even test them on the Facebook platform as ads and see which one sends the most clients your way.

The three main modalities of learning are auditory, kinesthetic, and visual. You're probably wondering what the hell all this means. Auditory is the message of words. Usually, it's using our ears, but writing is also an auditory learning mode. So the branding that we do is with our spoken and written words. Kinesthetic branding is the way that we make people feel. It's tactile and emotional. Finally, the third part of branding is visual branding; this is the way you appear to others and the way they see you.

Auditory Branding
As we develop a personal brand, we become really intentional with the words we use. I'm talking about the words we use in writing and on our videos and posted next to pictures online and even in the things that we share. Don't take this as permission to be fake. Being authentic is essential to a great personal brand. This is why it's so important that your words match up with the values you

stated earlier.

In addition to our words matching our values, our message has to be crystal clear and laser sharp. In high school, I really struggled with writing papers. I have no tolerance for filler. It's gotta be straight and to the point. If you struggled to write long papers that's good news. If you struggled in English in high school that's also good news. When we're delivering our messages, we don't want people to think that we are a bullshit artist. Get to the fucking point already! Remove as much business speak and insider language as possible in your auditory branding. Even if you're in a business-to-business focused personal brand, do as much as you can to stay away from business buzzwords.

Are you smarter than a fifth-grader? Probably not. Unless your niche is talking to a biochemist, your message should be clear for a fifth-grader to read or listen to. Consider how you could clarify your message, so even your fifth-grade nephew can understand.

If there is one thing that I hope this book can do for you, it's to help you find clarity and focus for your brand. In focusing your message, you will stand out among the crowd. You'll be an expert, not a generalist. You'll precisely say what you do, who you serve, and how your clients are at the core of your personal brand.

Kinesthetic Branding
Kinesthetic branding is the way you make your potential

clients feel. When someone meets you for the first time, how do they feel? Consider your handshake; is it like a fish, firm, or is it a death grip? Do you hug people? The tone of your voice can carry a feeling. If you're using a monotone voice, which is something that I struggle with, by the way, your clients might feel like you aren't excited. Show excitement in your tone, your body language, and your smile!

The Queen of Kinesthetic Branding is Vanessa Van Edwards. She explains in her book *Captivate*, and on her website, The Science of People, how to excel at kinesthetic branding.

Here's an exercise that you can do for kinesthetic branding. Give someone a handshake and get some feedback on the experience. The only acceptable handshake is pleasantly firm.

In your business, figure out ways to go above and beyond. You want your client to feel like a rockstar. This involves sending each client that spends significant money with you, a personal written thank-you note from your business. Whether you do this or someone else at your business does this, it's essential to send personal thank-you notes. If you can't take the time, hire a highschool student to hand write these cards.

Visual Branding
As a photographer, the visual brand matters a lot to me. When I work with clients for personal branding photo

sessions, I ask what they plan on wearing. When they don't know what they're going to wear, I set them up with someone who is an expert in this area. This is a service that Nordstrom offers for free, so if you're not sure where to go, visit your nearest location. They can have a personal shopper design your visual brand based on what you do.

If you are naturally a kinesthetic or auditory learner, you might struggle with this. Some people have signature clothing or jewelry they always wear. Your brand should visually appeal to your ideal client.

Your personal brand needs to be authentic. You don't need to rent a Lambo for your brand if you don't own one. If you are hyped up 100% of the time, people will think that you are unrelatable. They won't be able to connect with you or point to a reason why they can't. Therefore, as you craft your auditory kinesthetic and visual branding, make sure to occasionally talk about flaws or struggles. Do this without being negative. Ask questions and get help with certain things. When you don't know something, don't be afraid to say, "Let me find out an answer for you." The reason many people see old-school salespeople as defensive is they aren't authentic, that they pretend to know all the answers when they don't. In this new age of the internet, it's impossible to be inauthentic for too long. You will eventually get found out. Your client will write a review that will expose you for being fake.

Here's the funnest part of all: your personal branding photoshoot! If budget is a concern, begin with a really good professional headshot. You can expect to invest between $150-$500. Once you are further along in your journey, you need to invest in 10 to 30 personal branding images. This will represent you, your product, your service, etc. online via your website and social media platforms, as well as in print. You can expect to invest between $1,500 - $5,000 total.

I take clients through a journey of self-discovery to clarify their personal brand. They leave with a clear understanding of who they serve as well as great photos to appeal to their target audience, respectively.

If you are looking for a photographer, your friends may be able to offer you a referral. Especially if they've also had a similar experience. If you are sourcing your photographer from the Internet, make sure to seek out personal branding specifically, rather than a "one and done" headshot. When you call, they should have pricing information readily available for personal branding. (I know a guy www.allebachphotography.com)

Chapter 4

Designing Your Net: Finding and Catching Clients

Today I was on the phone with a client and they asked "How do you get everywhere? I've seen you on TV, Huffington Post, local newspapers, and in Cosmopolitan. How do you do that?"

The simple answer is, I pitch and throw my ideas out there. The longer answer is written in the pages to follow. You can get your own press! Like I mentioned earlier in the book, advertising is the tax for not getting press. The issue is not whether you can get press for your ideas and solutions to people's problems but who you are going to get to spread your message. This takes persistence. You'll need to be willing to stick to it. Some wins happen overnight and for some of my biggest wins, it's taken months or years.

In the words of Rob Schneider in the movie *Waterboy*, "You can do it!"

Now you know who you are and what you have to offer to the world. We've focused your message and defined your niche. Now it's time to deliver your message and tell your story. In the next exercise, you'll find out where your dream clients hang out, not only online but where they hang out in person.

Interview five of your favorite clients
Where you get your news from?
What are your most visited websites?
What is your favorite social media network?
What events do they attend?

Interview your clients in person or over the phone if possible. Since you are asking about social media preferences, you'll want to stay away from posting to social media to keep the results more accurate. Pick out your favorite clients and ask them where they hang out. If you are entirely new to your profession and don't have clients yet, imagine where your dream clients hang out. With my tattooed bride and tattooed wedding niche, I was able to advertise in an online publication called Offbeat Bride. This website was the critical factor in getting the perfect clients. Finding these places where your clients hang out are goldmines. When you find places where clients already buy into your worldview, they can convert into clients at a significantly higher rate than generic leads. If I had advertised in traditional wedding websites, I would not have not gotten the same type of clients.

Another tricky way to find out this information is to go on an Instagram profile and then down arrow your business profile, or an ideal client's Instagram, and you'll see the most similar type of accounts and businesses. Don't be afraid to search for Facebook groups that your clients might be in. Search your niche, and you'll be surprised to find groups may already exist. Use these groups for research. Don't be that spammy person. If no group exists, create one!

Approaching businesses and websites to partner or advertise on is one of the best ways to find your ideal clients. Say you are a realtor who specializes in houses with pools; you would want to look for companies that service swimming pools in your local area. Look for ways to partner and create opportunities for mutual growth and events that benefit both of you!

Social Networks
Viral personal brands must be on at least one social media channel. Start out by focusing on one social media channel, move to two, and, if you have time, move to three. After three social media channels, you'll start to spread thin. But before it's too late, capture as many of the social media channel names, so no one else can steal them. Just fill out the bio section, and your website if you're just reserving the space and the URL. Since going viral requires focus, please don't spread yourself too thin. If three social media networks sounds like too much, stick to one or two. Over the next few pages, I will explain how you can leverage social media. We'll examine the advantages and disadvantages.

Engagement is Everything
With social media and going viral, there is one constant.

Engagement is everything. Content must engage the followers, and you must also participate. The more people who engage with your content, the more people see it. This is at the heart of seeing social media virally. Ask yourself, "How can I get more interaction and participation on each post?" Almost all social networks use algorithms to see how popular content is. Popular content is shared with people outside of the followers of a particular page or person.

This interaction is a must; what good is it if you create all this wonderful content, and you aren't interacting with people? Posting without interaction on social media is time wasted. Until you've scaled so large that you're able to hire a part-time or full-time social media manager, you should try interacting with everyone on each post. Like their comments, respond to the questions, direct message them, and encourage them to take the next step!

How Often to Post
A simple social media plan can be one post on each network every day, five to seven days a week. This strategy works on most social networks (Twitter is about volume of posts, so it won't work there). I recommend finding a social media tool that will allow you to schedule in advance so that you are not breaking up each day looking for content and scheduling it. The software will figure out how many times to post to your social media automatically, taking the guesswork out of it. Choose one day every month to schedule all your content on social media. For scheduling, I recommend buffer.com

(schedules all social media accounts) or Tailwind, which handles Pinterest and Instagram.

As you experiment with posting, you'll find some networks will allow for more posting. Follow the metrics. Savvy personal brands experiment with the frequency of posts. If you see engagement dropping when you post more, post less. If you see engagement go up when you post more often, post more often. In my experience, if you have great engagement on your page, Facebook will show your posts to even more people if you post more.

Facebook
Facebook still is my number-one recommended site to grow and go viral on. It's still the most widely used social network out there. Currently, at the time of this writing, there are 1.25 billion users on Facebook.

Before we dive in, I need to explain the main elements of Facebook marketing.
- Personal Facebook Wall
- Facebook Groups
- Facebook Messenger
- Facebook Pages
- Facebook Live

Personal Facebook Wall
When you initially sign up for Facebook, this is what you see. This is your personal profile page, and this is where your friends wish you happy birthday and send you funny cat videos. Do your best to keep this 80% non-business

20% business. If you go too far in the business direction, you can be flagged for running a personal profile as a business. This can result in your personal account being warned or deleted.

The upside of your personal wall is it generally reaches the most people without paying; this is especially true if your Facebook page is really really small. You should be sharing the best 20% of your business content on this page. You shouldn't be sharing all your business content on this page because, as mentioned before, you can get your profile flagged.

The goal for social networks is to get people to know, like, and trust you so they can make the next step in their journey. Less than 20% of your posts on your personal profile should include Calls To Action (CTA) or include your website address. This would seem too salesy for your personal page.

Things to share on your person Facebook account
- Family Photos
- Cat and dog photos
- Memes
- Funny news stories
- Funny Videos
- Music Videos
- New Headshot
- Inspirational stories
- Big news for your business
- Events you are hosting

- Media appearances
- Sales for your business (sparingly . . . less than 20%)

Facebook Groups
Facebook groups around a niche or your business tend to have better engagement. Wouldn't you love if your clients helped you turn skeptical people into clients? Facebook groups do this for me! I use Facebook groups to convert people from fans to clients. Your client evangelists will convert people into clients. In my group, I love asking why people are afraid to have a photo experience. Skeptical people share their fears, and my clients automatically respond to them with their own stories.

Good things take time. On January 1st, I only had 30 members in my group, and no participation from those members. At the time of this writing, I have 2,200 members and 12,600 comments over the last month. The process took 11 months and a lot of work. In order for most successful groups to get going, you have to post to an almost empty room daily for several months. The daily action will get the results you are looking for. Your content for a Facebook group should be teaching and interactive. It's a great place to ask engaging questions related to your niche and your brand. These groups should have an element of fun to them to keep clients (and potential clients) coming back for more. In addition to fun content, this is a great place to run contests.

Invite people who like your page, friends in your niche, ideal clients, and potential future clients. Facebook makes it easy to add people to your group. Run Facebook ads to your current Facebook page members to join your Facebook group. Contests are another great way to get people in your group. Challenge people to invite 10 friends who'd benefit, randomly draw a winner, and give them a prize. Use Facebook's admin tool to welcome every new person into the group daily (This sounds so simple, but I should charge you $1,000 for this tip). Don't skip this step. You might as well not do Facebook groups if you skip this.

Currently, Facebook groups are much more likely to be seen by your clients because they are social. They are also the hardest to get going but can have the most payoff. We'll talk more about this in the last chapter on community.

Many posts in the group can go to over 100 comments. Don't just post about your business, though. Also, post anything interesting or helpful to your ideal clients. Post funny things. Post engaging questions.

Content to share in your group
- Silly questions based around your niche
- Compare and contrast questions (Is this better than that?)
- Answers to frequently asked questions people have about your product or service
- Feedback on new ideas
- Models & Beta testers for new products
- Giveaways and samples
- Events
- Client of the Month

- Videos you make yourself
- Facebook Live in your group
- Viral videos that fit your niche
- Other viral content
- Educating your potential clients on products or services

Facebook Pages: Get More Engagement than Apple
At the beginning of the year, I was frustrated with how few people saw my Facebook. While my Instagram pages were doing amazing, my Facebook remained virtually unseen. I believe Facebook pages are essential for all brick-and-mortar stores as well as personal brands. So I set out to find out what major brands were doing to make

Page			Total Page Likes	From Last Week	Posts This Week	Engagement This Week	
1	Nikon	Nikon	14.7m	▲ 0.1%	5	676	
2	BEST BUY	Best Buy	8.7m		0%	6	900	
3	SONY	Sony	7.9m		0%	12	5.6K	
4	Toyota	Toyota USA	4.2m		0%	10	4.5K	
5	Canon	Canon	1.3m		0%	32	1.8K	
YOU 6		Couples Boudoir Photo...	7.1K	▲ 2.4%	54	7.5K	

their pages successful. And I stumbled on something huge nobody is talking about.

Real talk, when I started writing this book, I only had 1,700 likes on my Facebook Page, Couples Boudoir Photography Guy. I'd average three likes on most posts.

It was embarrassing. At this time, I have over 7,100 likes/followers and more engagement than Apple. What is the difference that will make your page succeed?

Hitting that share button! Sharing other page's viral content is my secret to rapid growth. Before adopting this strategy, nobody clicked on the articles I posted. By sharing other page's visual and video content my page exploded. It's as simple as sharing other content your audience will find interesting. One post a day is a great place to start. The more people comment on and like your posts, the more posts you can run a day. My best performing page, Couples Boudoir Photography Guy, runs up to 10 posts a day. Outside of posts I share from other pages, my content is scheduled through a program called Buffer.

Ethically Steal Your Competitors Most Engaging Facebook Content

The breakthrough I had was watching different competitors and large brands to see what was working for them. Visit your Facebook Page, then click Insights. Once you're on Insights, scroll down to Watch Pages. Follow several large brands in your niche and a few brands matching your worldview and values. Click on the pages you are following, and it will show you their most popular posts. It can even benefit you to share content from your competitors. Hit the share button on a few you love!

This is the million-dollar hack. If you're looking for a way to get more reach without spending money, consider sharing viral videos and viral content. Find viral content matching your brand and hit the share button. These type of posts will get more shares and more reads than your other posts made by you. People will see this viral content you shared, and it leads back to you. So start hitting the share button on more content that matches your message. Future clients will see your name in their Facebook newsfeed over and over again. It's a way to build trust with your personal brand.

Facebook Messenger & Chat Bots
The most recent innovation in Facebook is Messenger. My prediction is messenger will become one of the greatest selling tools over the next few years. Using a combination of robots and humans, you can answer your clients biggest questions, and get them booked on your calendar in Facebook Messenger. This method allows for you to chat live with your potential clients, quickly answering basic questions.

Many Chat is the service I used to manage Facebook Messenger. It works in tandem with Facebook Messenger for your business. You can program (or buy pre-programmed) responses for your business's messenger to give answers on everything from pricing to contact information, scheduling, and frequently asked questions.

While installing a Messenger bot isn't necessary to get started, it will save you tons of time in the end. It will also make you appear available at all hours without actually having to be awake. The Messenger bot or Many

Chat Messenger bot will get the conversation started for you. If you are really advanced, you might be able to take your client through to purchasing or scheduling an appointment. This is the greatest innovation in social media marketing in the last several years!

Facebook Live
Facebook has a live video platform, allowing you to use video to livestream and interact with viewers. You can run a Facebook Live inside of a group, on your business page, or on your personal wall. Unless you have a huge following on your page or group, expect to get the most interaction on your personal Facebook wall. The number-one consideration is practice, practice, practice. Write a post-it note with your top points and the number-one thing you are going to address. Right from the get-go, you're going to engage your audience, letting them know what they're going to get, and why should they stick around. Unlike other forms of video content on a livestream, they may be coming late. Be sure to repeat where you are, what you're doing, and what's going on several times throughout the whole process. It will seem like you're repeating yourself a little bit, but for the benefit of new viewers, do this to let them catch up.

Example: Hi! This is Mike Allebach, and I'm here to talk about what to wear to a headshot photo session.

Then break that down into three separate sections. Most importantly, you're going to share a good client story or personal story. Since stories have been around since the beginning of time, they are often the best way to convey our ideas.

Ideally, you'll want to have a story for each of your three points in Facebook Live as well. As Facebook users log on, wave and engage with each of them if possible. If it's a really big group, you won't be able to engage with all the users, so a general welcome to everyone who just logged on is fine. The more you're able to engage with the people watching, the more they will engage and stay on. Ask questions and give responses with your audience. Make sure there is some reward for sticking around to the end. Give your audience a call-to-action with what are they supposed to do next. In a call-to-action, you'll share the way they can work with you next, buy your product, or get on a waiting list.

Another great type of Facebook Live is a "pull back the curtain, behind the scenes, show them how you do what you do" video. Give them a piece of knowledge they never had. Use the lever of intrigue to capture their attention. This is where you give them a really good behind-the-scenes look at what you do, and information they never would have known before. Some of my most popular posts have been industry secrets! My industry secrets are only secret because my industry peers were afraid to express themselves. Once I put my industry secrets out there, all the photographers in my industry wanted to share theirs, too. It wasn't information that hurt us; it was information that helped us. They can be funny things! Or just live video of you doing what you do best. Also, think about things in your personal life that might relate to your clients. If you are a mom, share mom centric ideas; if you are a part-time chef, share part-time chef centric ideals.

Facebook Remarketing Ads
This isn't a book on Facebook or Google ads. But they are important tools you need to know how to utilize optimally. Remarketing or sometimes called retargeting sends ads to people who have visited your website already. Think of when you visit Amazon to search for a product and don't buy it. Then you see these ads for the next month. That is remarketing. It is the least expensive and most powerful type of advertising out there. People who have already visited your website are the most likely to buy. They just need more follow up. Let Facebook remarketing do the trick to pushing them over the edge to becoming a client!

I recommend spending $1- $10 a day on remarketing ads. Start by installing the "Facebook pixel" on your website. This smart pixel links up the people who visited your website with their Facebook profile and runs ads to them. This is how Amazon and other retailers advertise to you when you look at a product.

For many niches, Facebook and Google are still the best dollar-for-dollar investment in ads. These may be the most powerful tools you have for finding and communicating with your niche. Facebook ads give you the ability to find clients by their age, gender, and interests. You have a huge opportunity here to communicate with only people who care about your niche. When an article or video I've worked on has first gone viral, I add fuel to the viral fire. I have personally used Facebook ads to assist articles in going viral. Once they get going and stay going, this really helps to increase communication to the small slice of people who really care.

After running an ad for a bit, Facebook will give you a relevancy score; you'll want to mostly run ads getting a 7-10 score. If you aren't getting at least a 5, you are usually missing the mark with your ad. Delete the ad, and start over if it's under 5. If it's over 5, tweak it and get it up to 7-10! Most of my ads are 9 or 10 because I know exactly what my clients love, and I've been testing ads for 10 years. This subject deserves its own course.

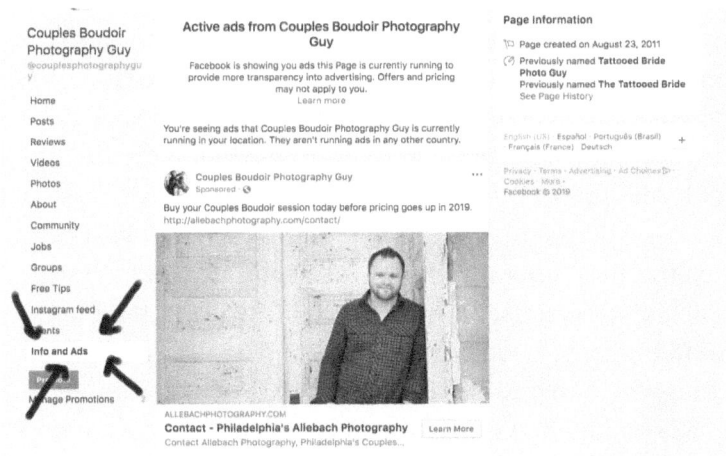

Stealing Ideas for Ads

Since big companies have huge budgets and test their ads,

it's great to take their tested ideas and apply them to our personal brands. Since the Russian Facebook ad scandal, Facebook has tried to provide a level of transparency with ads. This means you can see all the ads of major brands and even your competitors!

To view current ads, click the page and then click "Info and Ads." All of their current ads will appear. Viewing big brands' ads is a great way to help you think about creating successful ad campaigns. Start creating your swipe file of great ads today!

Viral Tip: Engagement
All social media channels give boosts to pages they see engaging with their fans. They use engagement to show more people what you are doing. So respond to every comment left on your page if only with a simple thank you or a call to action when appropriate. Engagement, engagement, engagement. Engage with your clients. Talk with them. Celebrate them. Send them cards. Post photos with pictures with their names on it. Retweet every positive mention on Twitter. Make your fans and followers feel like superstars. Make their day. Transform their lives. Send them gifts, send them cards, and be the person who cares when no one else does. I have an "average" budget of $25 per client. I want to spend $100 for my best clients and send handwritten cards to everyone. Doing this really makes everyone feel like a superstar.

YouTube and Snapchat
YouTube and Snapchat are the perfect places for visual

and service brands. Record how-to videos or explainer videos. Give daily behind the scenes. Show potential clients something they don't know about your business. Let's say you're a painter; you can show how certain painting techniques would be used in the home. By showing off your expert skill, you're answering their questions while, at the same time, creating interest in hiring you.

Another profession great for Youtube and Snapchat is a makeup artist. There are so many makeup artist showing off their skills, and many of them aren't very good. So if you are a professional makeup artist, you can stand out by doing video tutorials. We also have to think not only about potential clients, but that current and past clients are seeing these videos. Doing video tutorials shows that you're proficient and still the go-to person when they have future needs.

Youtube is the second biggest search engine in the world. If you are struggling to be on the first or second page of Google, try ranking on Youtube instead. You can rank on the first page of Youtube for a search phrase by carefully naming your video and typing your description. Video Marketing Blaster is a great software to help you rank videos on Youtube. It searches through the best videos, and figures out the perfect title for your video. Sometimes the titles are a bit nonsensical, so I make them easier to read.

People go to YouTube and Snapchat for entertainment

or to learn how to do something. If you can entertain or show how to do something you'll find new clients on these platforms.

Lastly, here's a note about audio. Audio is one of the most important pieces for making videos. Make sure audio is clear and easy to understand. Buy a better quality microphone for your cell phone if that's what you use. Microphones greatly help with audio quality. Some cell phones have two mics and are able to filter out background noise.

If you are using a computer, buy a simple microphone for your computer, and use a better quality webcam. I use the Audio-Technica ATR 2100 USB microphone. Also, hang blankets in the room if you have an echo; this is what recording studios do. If an echo is too bad, people will turn your Facebook live off.

The second most important consideration is good light. Find a continuous softbox lighting kit or a ring light. It doesn't have to be expensive, but make sure it's labeled "continuous lighting for video."

Client Video Testimonials for Social Media
I love the on-the-spot testimonial for Facebook and Facebook Live. This is the easiest way to get started with video. Just whip out your phone when a client is willing to give a testimonial or when you're doing a job. Let the client tell viewers what they got from the service or product and ask a few follow-up questions. Make sure

your client repeats your question in their answer.

My favorite client testimonial questions are:
- What was the main issue you faced before coming to us?
- How is life different since using our product or service?
- What are the benefits you experienced with our product or service?
- What would you say to someone on the fence about buying this?
- What made you choose us?

Twitter
Twitter is an important social media platform, but not in the way one might think. I recommend that everyone has a Twitter account for pitching. You don't have to use it regularly. Let's be honest, I mainly use Twitter for complaining about bad customer service and pitching to journalists.

When you want to grab the attention of a hard-to-reach journalist, reach out via Twitter if you are having trouble with normal channels. Same goes for big brands. You don't have to have a large following, follow journalists, brands, and friends so that you have a legitimate-looking profile and don't look like a bot. Put your real photo in there (remember that one you took a few chapters ago?) and fill out the description with your tagline and contact info.

Follow a minimum of 100 people who could write about your business. This includes every TV news reporter in your local market and publications and journalists in your niche markets.

Twitter is a great way to get in the news the next day. Within five minutes, you can tag multiple journalists with your tweet. Because Twitter isn't used as much as other social profiles, it's easy to get a hold of people on Twitter. When you want to cut through the noise, use Twitter. When you want to partner with someone or are trying to get your message out there, go to Twitter. Just last week, a friend of mine used this advice, posted a video, and tagged it in 10 different news organizations. His video went viral in a few hours and was played all over the United States

with his business tagged in it.

Sidenote: my favorite use for Twitter is to get better customer service. It's magical how social media people can get things done that other customer service people can't.

Twitter has become the place for breaking news. It's a

great place to find out what news is happening hours before it hits Facebook and other news outlets. It's a great to have this platform in your back pocket when you are trying to reach that hard-to-reach person.

Just like all the other social networks, you'll want to reply to every question you receive. Set up an alert on email inside of Twitter if you are rarely on, so you don't miss tweets directed at you!

Instagram
Right now, Instagram is on fire. Instagram has two ways of sharing pictures: posting to your profile or streaming live stories. Both are essential for IG Marketing. Uploading photos to your profile will post them indefinitely. Using this method, you can have virtually unlimited words on your photos to engage and inspire. The most engaging accounts take the time to write out meaningful anecdotes for their followers. This engagement creates awareness.

On the other hand, Instagram Stories are 24-hour posts. This is Instagram's answer to Snapchat. These are temporary posts, and as such they don't have to hold as much value. It's a great way to show off short little clips of things that you are working on with your personal brand. IG Stories can be pictures, boomerangs, or video. Unlike Facebook Live, you can watch your Instagram stories before you post them!

One of the newest features of Instagram stories is the ability to link them to a website. Customers can swipe up on your stories to go to your link. Currently, Instagram requires you have a business account with 10,000 or more followers. This feature allows you to sell directly from Instagram stories.

Share client testimonials on Instagram and Instagram stories! Show the success of your clients. Capture their stories directly to Instagram. If they mess up somehow, you can just re-record their testimonial. If your only take-away from this book is a collection of customer testimonials, I'd still call this a success.

Make your Instagram bio interesting. If you developed a nickname earlier, use this nickname as your username for Instagram. If you are using a tagline, that tagline should appear in your bio as well as your website. Keep your Instagram profile private until you reach at least 100 followers. Once you hit 100 people, your profile looks more legitimate, and people are more likely to follow you. Private profiles are good for quick growth as they will follow you because they can't see what's inside your profile. Don't stay with a private profile for long as people won't be able to search using hashtags on private profiles. Be sure to post potentially viral pieces of content to Instagram by changing the profile link in your bio for 48 to 96 hours.

Hashtags are the way Instagram sorts information by keyword(s). Many people explore Instagram by hashtags. For example, people can use #globalwarming to search for graphics or label graphics as being related to this subject.

Hashtags are good and will raise engagement but not as powerful as many Instagram coaches claim. Hashtag each post with a few niche phrases, geolocations, and generic keywords. I'd recommend 10 to 29 hashtags per post. Questions are a great way to create engagement along with the hashtags.

An engaging post for a New York City makeup artist might look like this:

"Created this new makeup look for fall. What do you guys think?

#golden #smokeyeye #goldeneye #goldensmokeyeye #macmakeup #makeupbrush #fall #autumn #MUA #HMUA #pumpkinspice #makeuptips #makeuptutorial #NewYorkCityMakeupArtist #NYCMUA #queens #manhattanmakeupartist"

Journalists also use hashtags to search for photos for stories. Don't be surprised if a journalist contacts you for permission to use a photo or graphic you created.

LinkedIn
If you serve business-to-business or salespeople, then LinkedIn might be your key social media platform. Many people have success building their brand on LinkedIn. As a photographer, LinkedIn hasn't been one of my key platforms. It does show up in Google search results, so if you sign up, make sure you fill it out completely. Include your nickname as your middle name on your bio. The

words in your bio section are accessible through a search on the website, so be as descriptive as possible, and make sure to include your tagline. Include a link to your website in your bio as well.

Pinterest
Welcome to the second-biggest image search engine, Pinterest. It's Google search meets bookmarking and scrap-booking.

Pinterest is perfect for interior designers and decorators and visual artists to show their work. Pinterest can positively affect search engine results for your business, it also helps signal Google to show your website in searches.

The viral formula for Pinterest is as follows: share 80% other people's work and 20% of your own. Pin 80% of friends and industry leaders into helpful boards. Pin 20% of your best content, photos, and articles. Use Tailwind to more easily share your content and schedule your pins.

Reddit
It would be a big miss to exclude Reddit from this book. The site is famous for quickly making things go viral. They look down on self-promotion, so the best way to have a shot at Reddit making you viral is to send your article to a friend who uses Reddit to post. I don't recommend using black hat or shady techniques on Reddit.

Quora
Shhh, I'm going to let you in on a major Google search

engine secret. Over lunch, many years ago, a friend let me in on a huge secret. Marketing and search engine optimization (SEO) companies use Quora for research. They dig through Quora to find the most commonly asked questions. They, in turn, create content around the commonly asked questions to guarantee they will show up in Google. If people are asking questions about it on Quora, they are searching for answers on Google. I use this technique myself. Start researching commonly asked questions in your industry. In addition to making videos, articles, and blog posts, answer the questions in Quora! In no time, you will be seen as a leader in the industry.

Both Quora and Reddit use upranking and downranking, putting the best answers and comments at the top of the thread. In addition to these sources, regular forums and groups are good places to learn about the temperature of your business and niche.

Google Alerts
If you care about your business or personal brand reputation, I'm sure you've typed your name into Google at least once. Thankfully, there is a better way to see all the stories and articles featuring your business in than googling yourself or, even worse, forgetting to. Set up a Google alert for your name and company's name. Also, set up a Google Alert for your niche. Google will then send you relevant articles as they are posted. This is the first thing any PR firm would do for you to help you manage your reputation.

Respond to articles and questions when appropriate. Remember, not all comments on the internet deserve to be read or commented on. Ignore the trolls. Instead, focus on helping people with real questions and provide answers.

Call To Action
In designing your client net, what should our client do next? How can they start working with you? How can they get their product?

If you are selling low-end products and services, you can simply put in a link to buy your product or service. You won't need a one-on-one meeting, seminar, or phone call to sell most $49 products.

Selling services and products over a thousand dollars is difficult without videos or phone calls. People want to know that they're picking the right person; they want to be able to hear a human voice on the other line or at least see a video. Talking to someone who is offering a service is almost like test driving a car. They can quickly tell if they're cut out for the job.

Mastering the Phone
The next step in building an ideal client net is a conversation. This conversation can happen over the phone, Skype, or with a webinar. The phone is still where selling high-end products and services is the quickest. A process that might take months or years to nurture over email or social media, you can close a sale on the phone in 30 minutes.

If you have phone fear, don't be afraid to hire someone to handle this for you (or get over your damn self).

The phone converts fans into dream clients. On phone calls, you can manage expectations, listen to the tone of voice, and ask questions in real time. What might take 20 emails, can take 20 minutes on the phone. The phone is a viral personal brand hack. The promise of this book is to get your dream clients. It didn't say I would sugar-coat it for you; you've gotta learn phone or video if you want to take your business to the next level.

The viral hack of the phone is asking questions and actively listening. The rarely used skill of active listening is what sells on the phone. The person who is asking the questions is in control. You want to maintain control of a phone call by listening and asking questions. The amature mistake most non-viral personal brands make is talking too much. The real key is discovering their situation. Listen closely and intently. People rarely feel heard and will pay hundreds or thousands of dollars to people who are excellent listeners.

When prospective clients won't pick up the phone, I schedule a phone call with them. Scheduleonce is the service I used to schedule phone calls with clients. It automates the scheduling process. It saves me several hours a month in back-and-forth scheduling emails and helps convert leads into clients.

If you want to get your personal brand to the next level, mastering the phone or Skype is essential. You'll have to reach out to reporters on the phone, and you'll have to with clients. You will also need to pick up the phone so that you aren't missing media outlets when you go viral.

I remember driving in my car one day when my phone rang. I pulled over and picked it up, and it happened to be the tabloid, The National Examiner. The tabloid was wondering if they could run a story on Tattooed Brides, and they asked if $1,600 was enough to pay for the story! They were offering to run a story solely on my business and pay me for it! In essence, they were offering to run a free advertisement in their tabloid for me and also pay for the images they used in the story. If I hadn't picked up the phone, I never would have gotten this opportunity.

Journalists have no time for people who don't answer or return calls, and neither do your clients! If you don't have time to answer your phone or hate the phone, find someone to do it for you. You'll miss out on opportunities if you aren't responsive. Don't fail in business because you are "scared of the phone." Now that you have this awesome way to serve the world, it's time to put on your adulting pants.

One-on-one
One-to-one or face-to-face are the most effective way to go from conversation to sale.

Here is a brainstorm of ways to have one-to-one

interactions:
- Having a booth in niche conventions
- Free estimates
- Networking groups
- Working with nonprofits
- Stopping by businesses
- Collaborating with businesses
- Visiting conventions

While phone calls are the most efficient way to convert people into clients, in-person might be the most effective. In some situations, especially local business, an in-person 30-minute consult is much more effective.

I use this to my advantage. My business focuses on the niches of tattooed people and tattooed couples. I exhibit at a local tattoo convention. Twenty-thousand people attend this convention, and I'm able to talk to them about what I do. This makes booking much easier.

The more direct approaches tend to have the best results for people with viral personal brands. Find your dream client by going where they hang out.

If you're exhibiting at a location where they're hanging out, you'll want to stand out. Use prizes, bright signs, or just being plain friendly to grab their attention. Don't be like other vendors who sit down and play on their phones. Be friendly! Remember, start conversations to get clients. You'd be amazed at how far a smile goes on a convention room floor.

Public Speaking
A shortcut to becoming a viral personal brand is public speaking. Whether you use webinars, seminars or group panels, you'll immediately be seen as the expert.

Wait! First I said get over your fear of the phone, and now I'm bringing in people's biggest fear: public speaking!

My first time speaking publicly, I was so nervous that my voice cracked like a middle-schooler. Crackling over my words, I barely made it through the presentation. Not to worry, speaking got easier for me, and it will for you, too. Start getting comfortable with public speaking at a BNI group, a networking group where you get to give a 30-second pitch every week. A few times a year, you get a five to 10 minute presentation. This would allow you to ease into public speaking. If you want to be a viral personal brand, this skill will come in handy. Sooner or later, someone will ask you to speak if you become a viral sensation.

Follow-Up Strategy
As they say, the fortune is in the follow-up. But what does that mean?

The giant trap of advertising and marketing is to get as many people caught in your net as possible. Tragically, many people focus in on the advertising and PR part of their business, and forget about their hot leads who haven't yet booked. How to get the client's through three major stages of knowing about you, liking you, and trusting that you are their solution?

In "the knowing," stage they probably haven't yet reached out and contacted you; they just know about you. They may have seen an ad online or heard about you in the news but haven't yet checked out your full website or talked to you.

When looking at your dream client net, this is at the top. Your goal is to catch them further in the net. You want them to move to the like or trust stage. Looking back on past clients, what made them move forward? Knowing these transitions is key. Ask your clients what helped them progress forward.

The next stage, the "Like stage," is when a future client, just as it sounds, likes you. They may have liked your Facebook page or just find you pleasant in person. The more you understand your niche and dream clients, the more likely this will happen with little effort.

For most, the hardest transition will come from "like" to the "trust" stage. Potential clients might trust you, but if you don't have a service or product they require, they won't use you. Not everyone who trusts you is ready to use your services or even has a need.

The good news is it's possible to work through these stages pretty quickly.

Long-form content is the hack. Your discovery phone calls, webinars, and in-person meetings all help transition your clients from unknown to known to like to trust. It's as simple as this: discovering their situation, answering their questions, calming their fears, and solving their problems.

Once these leads are in your CRM or email, you need a follow-up strategy for the ones who don't book right away.

An often-repeated phrase I say in the studio is "Follow up until people say FU." If people have requested info, I assume they still want info until they tell me otherwise. My minimum for following up is nine times.

This week, I finally booked a client who reached out over a year and a half ago. We've emailed and followed up over 20 times. He said, "Life sort of happened, and now we are ready to go through with a photo session. I lived in three different states over the last year and a half."

Lead Magnets and Landing page
The problem with many websites is they are too complicated. Clarifying your website so it's simple to use is a great strategy. Most people focus on getting traffic to their website. Smart people focus on converting traffic to buyers.

The easiest way to convert visitors is to send them to a landing page. It's a specific page you send potential clients to as a call to action in order to get them to contact you, or share their email address. The reason landing pages are so effective is they have no other menu items and nowhere else to go. It forces you to say to yourself either, "I'm giving my contact information to get more information," or "I'm closing this webpage."

Lead magnets are the way to trade email addresses in exchange for expert information from you. As you can never truly own a list of your followers on social media, it's wise to get people to sign up for an email newsletter. A lead magnet is a website that offers something free and helpful in exchange for your email address. In this exchange, you'll ask explicit permission to join your email list. I recommend Aweber to manage your email list. I use Aweber to keep things legal and organized for me.

Marketers gauge how successful landing pages are by their conversion rate. This is the rate of how many people take the next step, usually giving their email address or buying. The higher the conversion rate, the more successful a website is. Rather than being everything to everyone, the landing page is almost like a website's niche page. It gives a specific message and usually only has one or two buttons. Simplicity and clarity is everything. This page should have a few testimonials if possible. When you clarify what you want your potential clients to do, they do it more often.

Next Steps
It's been said that people buy from people they are friends with. Make potential clients feel like friends in any possible way. Make them feel like they matter by actually

listening, not just pretending to listen. Viral personal brand leaders are usually excellent listeners. At least, the kind of viral personal brand leader you'll want to be is a good listener.

Use the Ben Franklin effect to help propel people to take a next step. Ben Franklin would ask acquaintances, or people who didn't necessarily even like him, to borrow something like a special book from their library. By asking a favor from them, he would get into their circle of trust. In our mind, when we allow someone to borrow something, they are now a friend.

Many people will know about your personal brand or business; some people will like your business; a few will trust you and refer you, and the smallest chunk will buy from you. It's your job to figure out ways to get people to take the next step. It does you no good if a million people know about you, but nobody likes you, or a thousand people like you nobody trusts you.

Survey and chart what makes your clients take the next step.
Next steps:
- Lead magnets
- Email newsletters
- Forums & Facebook groups
- Live seminar
- Webinars
- Long form videos
- Physical mailers

- Testimonials
- Reviews
- Limited time offers
- Major piece of press

Seminars and Webinars

In a seminar or webinar, you are the expert. Or you are on a panel of experts. A seminar is a live, in-person model, while a webinar is the same thing but with the use of technology. You might have an audience asking questions live, or you might go through a slide presentation and videos. What a powerful way to share your expert advice with people! Your seminar should focus on only one problem facing your potential clients.

The formula I use for almost every seminar I give is focus on one problem. Have three steps to solving that problem. Each step will have one to three stories of how I solved this problem for myself or a testimonial of a client. The ending should show how you can help them solve the problem for them.

Testimonials and Reviews

Sharing testimonials and reviews is a good way to get people to take the next step. Once unbiased people have used your product or service, their words and stories become more powerful than yours!

The more you know your message, your values, and what your client express as their problems, the better you'll be able to craft questions for testimonials.

Business Partnerships
In 2014, I photographed tattoo artists at the Philadelphia Tattoo Convention, and it netted me 2000 new Instagram followers in one weekend. They shared my photos and tagged me in them. Although a simple reminder, partnering directly or indirectly can have huge results. The best partnerships go beyond social media into the real world. Who are some local businesses you could partner with? Who are some national businesses you can reach out to?

Over the years, one of my other great partnerships is a website and blog called Offbeat Bride. This website advertised to my specific niche of tattooed weddings and "offbeat" clients that make their own path to success.

While you don't want all of your eggs in one basket, partnerships can provide some businesses with most of their clients.

Getting Press
Getting press is the biggest word-of-mouth accelerator. When you ask people where they get business from, many will say word of mouth. Getting press for your business is like dumping gasoline on the fire of word-of-mouth. People trust news sources for trends and local business stories more than paid ads. The secret of getting press is knowing that journalists are looking for interesting stories from people like you. Journalists need you as much as you need them! The art of pitching your personal brand to

producers and journalists is easy, but takes a bit of faith. Not every pitch will land. Not every idea will fly. It's an art, a science, a skill, but, most of all, a numbers game. The more you pitch, the more stories you'll get, and the better your pitches will become. When you pitch, you are helping a journalist or producer do their job!

Getting Contact Information for Journalists
In many cases, the contact information for journalists is listed at the end of the articles they write. You should look at one recent article they've written before pitching. The other method is using Twitter, Linkedin, or a PR database. I personally use a discount database called Anewstip. Most databases run around $400 a month; Anewstip is $99 and saves me tons of time. It also allows me to pitch directly to journalists and see if they read the email. If you are serious about getting press, you'll want to sign up for a service like this.

Alternatively, there is a plugin for your internet browser called getprospect.io, and it allows you to find 50 email addresses a month through LinkedIn. They find the naming conventions and use databases to search for the real email addresses of almost anyone.

The Viral Pitch Formula
Every good pitch contains four things: a hook, an angle, timing, and the appropriate audience. Beyond this, it takes a dash of luck, follow-up, and people skills. That's why, in the pitching world, playing often is better than playing seldom or not at all.

Is pitching like boxing or fishing? Honestly, it's a little of both. The hook is what grabs the journalist's or producer's attention. Keep email pitches to around four sentences. It forces you to get to the point. A pitch is delivered to invite a conversation or interview. It isn't meant to give the whole enchilada. It's a tease. Get them to want more. Make it delicious.

This formula for me came from trial and error. Remember journalists are busy. They appreciate brevity and clarity in pitch emails.

Subject line: Curiosity or Just The Facts Hook?
Your pitch might go straight to the trash if you don't write a good subject line. The subject line should either be super direct, full of facts, or hit the curiosity trigger. The curiosity trigger is what both newspapers and clickbait sites use to get you to click. Large newspapers would employ a person just for newspaper headlines in the 20th century. Take your time crafting the title. A bland, straight-to-the-point subject can work for journalists, but sometimes a curiosity title can work as well. Make them want to click on your email to find out what is inside.

Sentence One: Introduction & Flattery
The introduction or flattery portion is a sentence about where you saw their work; if you are doing a personalized pitch, you're going to want to find people who've written on a similar topic before. This introduction is great for your first pitch. This says you know their work and proves

you know their audience. Introduce yourself and let them know where you saw their work, and, if you love the piece, let them know that, too.

An introductory email might go a little something like, "John, I saw your article in the New York Times on smart dog bowls and loved it, and I wanted to show you something I think you'll like."

The Pitch's Big Hook
The second sentence is your hook. Grab their attention! This shows the problem people are facing. Use story if you can. The secret to designing the perfect pitch is getting in the journalist's shoes. Take a look at a few articles they've written and find out some general info about them. Figure out what they might be motivated by. Trust your intuition. Try slightly different angles for each journalist you pitch to.

"At three months old, my dog choked on a mid-sized dog treat, and I had to do doggie heimlich and chest compressions to save Fido."

Social Proof
The third sentence is your social proof and solution. It's hard breaking a new story if no one else has. A journalist's credibility is on the line by sharing your story. If you can show this has been covered before, it will help. If this has been featured anywhere else, link to the article, or tell them about the number of shares on Facebook or on Twitter already if the number is substantial. If this is your first pitch, you won't likely have anything to put here, so

don't worry about it.

"I developed a choke-proof treat compatible with smart bowls that has been sold in over 126 stores in our region and featured on ABC7."

Call-To-Action Sentence
The last sentence is your call to action. This is where you show the best way to contact you and your cell phone number. Journalists and producers want to work with people who are easy to work with. They are under big deadlines and need you to answer your phone.

"Reach out to me today, and I can send you over the full press release, or call me on my cell phone at 215-555-5555."

I've mentioned this before, but get over your fear of the phone. If you want a viral brand, you'll need to get over your fear and deal with it. When pitching, you'll get calls from random area codes, so pick them up right away. If it's a spambot or telemarketer, hang up! It might be the New York Times calling for a quote. Clear out your voicemail before sending pitches, so anyone you do miss will get callbacks ASAP.

First, send pitches to local news, niche publications, or high-volume publications desperate for stories. Publications like international tabloids, although not highly regarded, are great places to get a start; so are your local newspapers. Getting a story in the bag is important for social proof in your following personalized pitches.

If you get national coverage, circle back to get local coverage after your featured. Local journalists don't want to miss out on a national story from a local person.

Journalists don't have time to reach back out to everyone who pitches. Don't expect to get replies from many journalists. The timing aspect of pitching is random, based on holidays and slow news days. Pitching is a game of both luck and skill. If the audience is right, a "no" from a journalist is usually just a "not now." You can pitch again in a month.

Years ago, I wanted to be featured in a certain magazine in my tattoo niche, and it took me sending pictures every six months for three years to get featured. I got my feature. So stay positive, helpful, make the journalist's job easy, and keep on pitching. Get inside the journalist's mind. They are working a job of high volume, and it's difficult for them to reach all their deadlines. Show yourself as a timely professional and don't give up. Just as the squeaky wheel gets the grease, the person who reaches out consistently eventually gets published (as long as they are respectful, helpful, and kind).

Do not act needy at any point. Nobody wants to help a needy business person. It's not attractive. Use intrigue instead. There is a fine line between stalking and following up. Don't send pitches every day. Don't get defensive or write mean emails or ask why they haven't featured you.

Keep press releases and pitches to once a month or less. Showing up is half the battle. The odds are in your favor. Practice, practice, practice your pitches. Make sure you personalize each one for the best result.

As you build up contacts, make sure that you keep them in a folder in your email. You can reach out to the best contacts over and over again as the years pass with new stories. Your best contacts will pick up your story almost every time. The best way to thank journalists is to write a handwritten thank-you note and send it in the mail. If you don't have an address, email a thank-you note! This will keep you top of mind.

Twitter Pitching
Always start with phone pitches for TV or email pitches for everyone else. Twitter is another way to pitch after you've gone through phone and email pitches. Welcome to the world of what is happening right now! When there is breaking news, this is where to pitch. Email addresses can be hard to find, but twitter accounts are not. This is another way to cut through the noise. Only the best stories make it through on Twitter. Expect this to be the least effective way to pitch, but if you have a breaking story, Twitter is the fastest way to get on the 10 o'clock news.

Search "assignment desk" in Twitter plus your city name to find where to tweet. These are where the television news producers interact with local breaking stories. Some stations only have one main account. In this case, tweet to the main account. Also, follow all your local reporters and newspaper journalists on Twitter. You don't need a big following on Twitter to make this effective, so don't worry if you only have a few dozen followers. Your pitch is what's important. You really only have to have two sentences and one picture to make it count.

TV Pitching
Prior to pitching a segment or event, put together a one-page PDF. You'll want this one-page document or PDF ready, so you can email it to the segment producer while you're on the phone. They will confirm that they received it while you are talking with them to ensure you it was received.

Your PDF document should include a bit about the segment or event and should include a picture of you in your brand outfit. Television loves visuals, so don't be afraid to go a little cheesy with the outfit you work in. Make the photo visually interesting. It shouldn't be a headshot. It should be an environmental portrait of you working or a white photo of you in your work attire. If you're a doctor, wear a lab coat; if you're a makeup artist, wear a makeup smock. If you are a baker, ham up your uniform. The picture alone may be enough to get you on the news. Make sure this photo is professionally taken.

The PDF should also include your contact information, including your cell phone, business address, or the town you reside in if it's a local segment, and your website and email. It should also have a simple, one-paragraph About Me/bio section. If you've been in the news before, it should mention where and when.

There's two different ways to pitch a TV station. The most effective for breaking news or upcoming events is picking up the phone to call the producer or the assignment desk. The assignment desk is what TV news uses as their switchboard for breaking news. If you have an upcoming event, call if you can. This is like a job interview, in a sense, if the producer answers. They will automatically be considering if you can be reliable on TV for an interview.

The important thing to remember when calling into an assignment desk is that usually you'll get someone who is not the producer. You are getting a gatekeeper. It's this person's job to see if you really need to talk to a producer. They're not necessarily well-paid or super experienced. Talk to them kindly and use your hook as the case for getting TV coverage.

Newsjacking
Newsjacking is what professional PR people use to get their clients on the news. Bend the narrative of your story to meet a current news story. This is a great way to be seen as an expert in your niche. Give an opinion on the current news, or have an interesting take on the current news. Think of any news story or holiday coming up and think of how your business or service relates. As always, this is a numbers game. Reach out for these types of segments annually in your profession, be personable, and you will eventually be on TV.

These segments are not segments to sell yourself. If you have written books or a wonderful website, they may decide to send your clients to buy the book or the website if it makes sense based on your segment. They may just introduce you as author of XYZ book, which can cause people to search for your book while they're watching television.

Making a video for your business costs usually anywhere from $2,000 to $5,000 plus, but getting on the news is free. There are sites where you can buy your news clip for $12-$200, saving you thousands. You can also use this clip on your website to sell your product or service.

Press Releases
A press release contains a headline, dateline, opening paragraph, body paragraph, boilerplate (optional), contact info, and the 5 W's.

Headline
Has the elements of pitches. It should hint at the subject without giving all the information away. The goal is to get someone to read the press release. I recommend writing out 25 versions of each headline and then picking the best one. I use Headline Analyzer to help figure out what the best headlines are:
https://coschedule.com/headline-analyzer
https://www.aminstitute.com/headline/index.htm
If it takes you as much time to write your headline as it does to write the press release that is normal. It's more important that you take the time to do it correctly. The

best headlines grab you emotionally and logically at the same time. There is also a curiosity hook that draws you in.

Dateline: City, State, Month, Day, Year.
Yes, this is as simple as it sounds!

Opening Paragraph:
Tell them what you're going to tell them, but leave them wanting more.

Body Paragraph:
Go through the 5 W's: who, what, when, where, why. Sometimes including client quotes.

Who: The people that we should be paying attention to, or the company that has released an innovative technique or idea. Who are the people this company serves? Without a clear "who," there is no story, no character to interview for a news story, and nothing to write about.

What: The thing being done. The product being released. What are these people using to get a better life? What are people using to thrive in their lives?

Where: Some stories are local, national, or international. Where does this story take place?

When: Past, current, or future?

Why: Providing a good result, or why this is happening, a feel-good story. Let news outlets know why we are providing such an awesome outcome. This is a place where we can share our own hero's journey. Or even better, we can make the clients the hero of the story, and share their journey.

Boilerplate (optional): General information about the company. Share the tagline, your purpose, or your mission in a succinct fashion. I don't always use this step.

Contact: Use your personal cell-phone number and your best email. Over the next month, you need to answer every call that comes in on your phone, just in case.

Writing and Distributing Your Release
If this is something you don't feel like doing, E-releases or a similar company can handle the writing for you. The benefit of press-release service is that you get to reach a large number of journalists quickly without sending a lot of emails. This service reaches out on your behalf to deliver the press release that you have crafted. This is great for events or new releases or when you've spotted an industry trend that you can speak to.

Some news websites will reprint your article without changing anything, which is called a press-release pick-up. Others will directly quote most of your article because they are under extreme pressure to create as much content as possible for their website.

Press releases aren't the first step that I recommend. The reason for this is they are like a shotgun approach. Press release services send to hundreds of news organizations, and some of them will put it on their website unchanged, and a few may reach out to you for more information. Writing a good press release is more advanced than writing a four-sentence pitch.

Press releases are up to a page (generally about 400 words) and include a lot of the same information but with a little bit more depth. Once you've had success with a pitch, expand the information to make it into a press release. You can pitch and never write a press release in your life. I suggest getting your press releases professionally written so that you don't have to learn the skill. Just send them the same four-sentence journalist pitch, and they'll interview you for the information that's missing.

Nickname Hack Revisited
We started off the book with an idea to give yourself a nickname. In addition to fun outfits and costumes for your professional brand, journalists and producers love nicknames. Once you use it yourself in a press release or pitch the journalist, they might publish it or pick it up. You can then say "XYZ Publications calls me the leader of XYZ niche."

Not everybody feels like a nickname is appropriate. So use this viral hack with care. If you are in a more traditional marketplace, it may not be advisable to use this tip.

Chapter 5

Creating Viral Content

I remember sitting around a fire roasting marshmallows and drinking beer with some friends, and we looked at each other and said "this story needs to be told." My friend, Jaleel, at the age of eight, became a victim of gun violence. A neighbor heard kids lighting off firecrackers and grabbed a shotgun. He fired it at the group of children hitting Jaleel. The shotgun pellets destroyed one of his kidneys, a quarter of his right lung, and part of his liver. Ever since, he has spent his life in a wheelchair.

Through his ups and downs, he has been honest with his story. Jaleel's resilience and tenacity as a photographer in a wheelchair has always inspired me. As a few friends and I sat around a campfire, I made a plan to tell the world his story.

I called Jaleel up and told him about my plan to tell his story through video. I bought a $15 mic from Radio Shack and met him to record the video. Among the hustle and bustle at a Sushi Restaurant, I put his story to video. If I knew what was to follow, I would have rented a studio to video his story.

After we finished the interview, I went home and edited the video and put it on Youtube. It was Oct 1, 2012, and I had yet to have any videos that spread virally. After putting it on Youtube and sharing it with friends, it took off. Within a few days it was shared over 1,000 times all over the world and was picked up by all the major photography websites. While I never made a dime on the video, it changed the trajectory of Jaleel's life and mine.

When people ask about the impact of viral and personal branding, I always go back to this. Jaleel's story was inspirational to thousands. One of the fan letters sent to Jaleel included a story of a man who was writing a suicide note, who saw Jaleel's video and credited it with saving his life.

In 2017, Jaleel won Sony's Impact Award. This video opened the doors for Jaleel and me to share his story from the stage. Jaleel has inspired audiences from all over the world in the last five years. It also has given the two of us many speaking opportunities.

If I hadn't listened to that voice saying this story needs to be told, my life would be much different. I would have never been asked to speak. The impact of viral stories can change your life and the lives of others.

If you've been in the corporate world, you've heard someone blurt out, "Let's make a viral campaign." If only it were that easy. There are no guarantees in life or in the viral realm. But there is a framework, a way to look at crafting content with the best chance of going viral. Even some of the greatest minds on this subject matter get baffled from time to time. Nobody bats at 1,000 in this field. No matter how great your ideas seem to you or your friends, they might not have the viral lift. What I want to teach you is some of what I've found that has worked for me and other people I know.

The more content you create, the more you talk on social media about your mission and your values, the more you'll see what is connecting with your audience. Crafting viral content starts with knowing your audience and knowing your industry.

It's helpful to follow other niche leaders in your industry to get ideas on subjects people are interested in. It's even more helpful to see what things aren't being discussed.

Triggers for Sharing Online
Every piece of viral content either educates, entertains, or engages. People share educational pieces to inform, and these pieces can hit both our mind and hearts. Entertaining pieces tell stories or surprise us. Engagement pieces ask us to interact, asking us to share our answers back.

In the early 1980s, Robert Cialdini discovered influence is based on six key principles: reciprocity, commitment and consistency, social proof, authority, liking, and scarcity. Take a break from this book and type "science on persuasion" into YouTube to understand his work in about 10 minutes. Putting the word "share" in your post will create another mental trigger for sharing. The more you hit Cialdini's mental sharing triggers, the more your content will be shared.

The Headline

Headlines can make or break an article or video. Create 25 headlines as quickly as possible before commiting to one. This process only takes 10 minutes if you allow yourself to create bad headlines. In ideation, we allow ourselves to write things without judgment. Start with silly or stupid headlines first. Once you allow the bad ones to be written, you'll have space for good headlines. Headlines for videos and articles should either direct us to engage, or intrigue us to click. Use the same headline scoring tool to help you figure out what headlines might connect the most with readers or viewers. Emotional words and numbered lists tend to get the most eyes.

I use the list from Buzzsumo's article "We Analyzed 100 Million Headlines. Here's What We Learned (New Research)" as a Bible to what headlines could be viral when I'm having trouble crafting headlines.

The Lead Photo

This can also make or break an article before it's shared or read. In the context of a video, this is the video thumbnail. Pick images that stand out or create curiosity. If you are serious about making the most viral content, you may want to run test ad campaigns to try out headlines or a few different photos. Spend $10 on each of your top three options for a headline, and share them on Facebook Ads and see which one gets the most votes. Choose the most likely to be clicked ad headline and photo.

Four Major Types of Potentially Viral Content to Create for Social Media
- Helpful
- Social Signaling
- Emotional
- Unexpected

Helpful Content
"This is pretty handy. I didn't know that!"

Go back to Quora for a big gold mine of free information. Craft videos and articles out of the questions people ask in your industry.

Another place to search is using Google's Keyword Planner tool. Type your niche into Google's free tool. You'll be able to see what people are searching for and the volume of searches. You'll want to look for things that aren't searched all that often or have little competition. You can rank number one in your articles for them. They will also be more likely to get shared in your industry. If you can help people solve problems and get what they want in life, they'll return the favor by using your business.

Other ideas for viral content include commonly asked questions in your industry. Use your F.A.Q. as a guide for this content. What are the most common questions you are asked? Can you make a simple Youtube video explaining this for your whole industry?

Top-10 tips also fall under the helpful category. Is there something in your industry that everyone talks about behind-the-scenes but nobody speaks of out loud? Are there secret hacks in your niche no one shares? Sometimes I write articles that look like they're meant to be read by brides, but I'm actually writing for photographers. By reading the minds of photographers, my message gets spread by other photographers. I'm writing articles with viral success built in. You can write for both your future clients and your colleagues who are spreading information their clients know.

Some of my best successes are because my competition shares my articles for me! If you make their job easier, they will help advertise you! How crazy is that?

Social Signalling
"Hey, we are alike in our worldview!"

Social signaling is a way to raise your status in your group of friends. Just as having a better car than your peers is a social signal, so is sharing certain types of content. When you have a community, take a stand for something you believe as a community! Be empathic, fascinating, and unique. The reason why most businesses people don't stand out is they aren't willing to. Define who you are publically. Most people aren't willing to publicly say what they stand for as a company, or what they stand against.

Whether you agree with the message or not, Nike did this

with their 2018 campaign when they said, "Believe in something. Even if it means sacrificing everything."

Most brands are so afraid of losing potential clients that they don't specify what they do. You become unique and fascinating by intersecting those two worlds.

Stand up for your client's worldview and you might take some hits. Make sure your ideals help your clients have a better world. Stick to subject matter most of your client base already agrees with you on, and they will share it. It can be serious or funny, and they will use it to raise their social status.

Emotional
"That hit me right in the feels."

Tap into the human narrative and emotion. Stand up for a human or a story. Let your clients get angry enough at an injustice to raise money for a cause. Let narrative guide you. Use your client's success stories as tales of your business's myth. Their story should have an overarching theme that matches your worldview.

What are their secrets struggles? What are their deepest desires, their biggest dreams, and how can you help them get there? How can you talk about how they feel? How can you talk about the ways they struggle empathically?

If you can help your future clients get what they want, they, in turn, will start to share what you have to say. To write or create videos, you'll need to get deep inside the minds of your clients and colleagues. Hit them right in the feels.

Be Unexpected
"Wow. I wasn't expecting that!"

Over-delivering to your clients is a great way to create viral opportunity. Obviously, this method relies on your clients to talk about you. This creates opportunity for your clients to tell a viral story about their experience with you!

Undersell and over deliver any way that you can. I mail Polaroid photos with messages to clients randomly. Sometimes we mail shirts or personalized gifts. Anything I can do to surprise and delight my clients creates social media stories they share.

Support your clients causes and silent auction gift certificates. Hand deliver products sometimes. Throw parties. Make them feel like they are a part of something larger. Invite them into your club. Be grateful and let them know how big of a part of what you do they are.

Do the unexpected. Be random. Do something not required by your industry or something even slightly weird.

Looking to really wow your client? A whole book could be written on this topic. In fact, the best resource I've found on this type of activity is *Never Lose a Customer Again: Turn Any Sale into Lifelong Loyalty in 100 Days* by Joey

Coleman.

Promoting Your Content to Go Viral

Send your content to your email list of subscribers. If possible, message to a few of your best friends or brand ambassadors to share. Everything you post should already show that it's been retweeted or shared already. This is social proof before anybody else sees it. So if you post something on your business page, use the share/retweet button to send somewhere else. People don't want to share unless they know other people have already shared it.

Your website should also show a like/share count. Install a plugin on your website if you don't already have one. This is more social proof.

When you are trying to assist an article or video going viral, you share it three times. Share it once, then, if it's getting a lot of attention, share it again three days later with a message about how many people have shared the article. This social proof is dynamite. Spend up to $100 in Facebook advertising to your target audience over the first three days. You can use your Facebook page's audience to create a 3% lookalike audience. Spend $100 advertising to your 3% lookalike audience.

Post your article in any groups you manage and any pages you own. Set your post to public on your own wall and make sure your Instagram and Twitter accounts are public as well. If you have a private Twitter or private Instagram, your content will rarely go viral, if ever.

Link each channel of social media together for the best chance for success. This will allow you to share from Instagram to Facebook and Facebook to Twitter.

In Twitter retweets, retweet everyone who tweets your article. For Facebook, like every person who shares your article. If you have time, also comment, and thank them for sharing the article. The more engagement around a piece of content the more likely it is to get seen. This idea is consistent with all social media. These platforms look for social signals, and personal engagement is the most powerful. Engaging will give content a bump to the top when people are interacting with it.

Your community will help you spread your message. Share your content in Facebook groups you manage, and, if allowed, in Facebook groups of your peers.

Viral Video Formula
Great videos start in the middle of the action. They grab the viewer's attention and create intrigue in the first three seconds. Resist the impulse to set the story up or tell the back story. The internet does not have time for this. We've all met the uncle who tells grand stories at the Thanksgiving table and quickly loses everyone's attention. Don't be this person. Grab the viewer's attention within three seconds or less. Explainer and hype videos, such as what In The Know and 60 Second Docs produce are a killer way to spread your message. They put lots of text

on the screen because most users watch videos on social media with the sound turned off.

Take notes from current TV series where they review what happened last week; this allows you right back into the story with a teaser. Great stories aren't always told chronologically; they usually are told from the middle. When you're telling your story, jump right into the action. You can always back up and deliver information that clarifies missing bits of information.

Your First Launch Formula
People often ask me, "Where do I start if I have an idea or product I want to launch?" If at all possible, start with a launch event or grand opening! This gives you the most potential for press, your friends, past clients, and community to get involved.

One of my favorite mantras is "Do the best with what you have." I'm going to lay out a checklist, but know you don't have to do everything on the checklist to have a successful event or launch. Let's use this to put all the pieces together. I've starred non-negotiables.

[ ] Clarify why you do what you do*
[ ] Define unmet needs and wants of dream clients*
[ ] Define who your target dream clients are*
[ ] Set a date and time for a live event
[ ] Press release to live event created
[ ] Facebook or Evite event created
[ ] Friends, family, clients, and future clients invited

[ ] Run ad for your event two weeks straight at a minimum of $1 to $10 a day to your biggest fans, leads, and 3% lookalike audience
[ ] Post to all relevant social media platforms
[ ] Call and invite TV three days before and the day of
[ ] Pitch to local newspaper and online press three days prior
[ ] Pitch to magazines two to four months out depending on size of magazine
[ ] Video promo about new product/service
[ ] Shoot video/photos during event and submit to press and TV next morning
[ ] Create takeaways people will want to post online

Test, Track, and Repeat
Each social and ad platform has tracking. Your website has ways to track how people are finding you, and what pages they are clicking on the most. This data is invaluable. Rather than try to cram a whole book's worth of knowledge here, I'm going to suggest two things...

I love and use Buffer to schedule many of my pieces of social media content. Buffer is great because it's simple and quick to use. If software isn't easy, you probably won't use it. Buffer also tracks the best pieces of content for you. Use their software to see what's most popular. Share your most popular pieces of content again and again!

If you are new to tracking your effectiveness, check out the *Conversion Code* by Chris Smith. It's the best book I've read on getting people to click on and buy what you are selling on the Internet. It gives the information on the best days and times to call, plus what methods to use to get people to book your services online.

Chapter 6
Creating a Tribe: A Community of Belonging

"People will do anything for those who encourage their dreams, justify their failures, allay their fears, confirm their suspicions, and help them throw rocks at their enemies."
- Blair Warren

The final piece to creating a viral personal brand is gathering the tribe. Or simply finding the tribe and leading it. There is nothing more powerful to your cause than 1,000 loyal fans and followers.

"To be a successful creator, you don't need millions. You don't need millions of dollars or millions of customers, millions of clients or millions of fans. To make a living as a craftsperson, photographer, musician, designer, author, animator, app maker, entrepreneur, or inventor you need only thousands of true fans."
- Kevin Kelly

Read Kevin Kelly's viral piece "1000 true fans" from 2008 here: https://kk.org/thetechnium/1000-true-fans/ . It's as applicable 10 years later as it was then.

Both Kevin Kelly and Blair Warren understood small tribes

of people, and tribe leaders working together make the difference in their community. We don't need a million followers. At this time, I have 2,300 people in my online community and 7,100 following our Facebook page, and yet we have more Facebook engagement than Apple! At the core of it, we are creating a place where like-minded people can take a step toward their truest and best self.

In 2013, Seth Godin released a tiny PDF called People like Us Do Things Like This where he said:

"For most of us, from the first day we are able to remember until the last day we breathe, our actions are primarily driven by one question, 'Do people like me do things like this?'

People like me don't cheat on their taxes.
People like me own a car; we don't take the bus.
People like me have a full-time job.
People like me want to see the new James Bond movie."

People operate in groups of people who are like-minded and who they can see a part of themselves in.

At the beginning of this year, I set out to finally bring the tribe I've been creating together into a centralized online community. I chose the easiest platform for me and just started working at it. In the beginning, it was a bit like talking to myself in a stadium. I just heard a lot of echoing while yelling, "Is anybody out there?"

That's the thing about lots of tribes. People wait for others to chime in first. People wait until they feel safe. People wait to follow. They have questions. What are the rules? What are the standards? Who is cool and who isn't? What happens if I break the rules? What happens if someone else breaks the rules in a way that hurts me?

If you've ever tried to run an online group, here is how it will work for most people. You'll post twice daily for six to nine months to crickets. At some point around six months, you'll get a little bit of response. After that, it will grow. Follow the 80/20 principle. Again, we want to engage and talk about others most of the time. Eighty percent should be entertaining or engaging, and 20% should be educational about you. If you rise to about 20% for education or sales, your group will be seen as spam and not community. It won't take off. The group will suffer with failure to launch.

Great communities grow slowly until they reach a tipping point. Once you hit the tipping point, they will start growing rapidly. Your job as a leader is to create space and ask questions. Good communities and tribes have leaders who lead with a gentle hand and create conversations.

"Friendship is born at the moment when one person says to another 'What! You too? I thought that no one but myself…"
- C.S. Lewis

The greatest shortcut is empowering your best clients to be evangelists and work on your behalf. Thank them immensely behind the scenes. Thank them publicly. Build in methods for them to be evangelists and spread the word. Make it easy. Make it a part of the process. Send them surprises in the mail. Create swag and products like shirts, stickers, mugs and such to show people they belong to the group.

Much of what I've learned about community has come from being in a punk-rock band and from the book by Peter Block called *Community: The Structure of Belonging*. This is why I use the same method of punk-rock bands, stickers, and T-shirts to help bring the community together.

Peter Block addresses empowering your community to make choices for themselves in his book. A light handed approach with your moderation online and allowing your community to self police is a great way to handle this. Let the community make the rules. As they define something as inappropriate behavior, add it to the rules of the group. Be a benevolent leader.

The six Conversations of a Community According to Peter Block:
1. **Invitation** - The ability to self-enroll into your community. We invite people to be a part of a community and a conversation about community. Whether you have an online forum or something that exists offline, this is a call to an alternative future.
2. **Possibility** - The idea that tomorrow can be a tiny bit different from today. We ask what is possible. How

can we change the status quo in the little slice of the world?

3. **Ownership** - The ownership conversation asks the question, "How have we contributed to the current reality? In this day and age, ownership is a bit of a foreign concept. It's important to ask how people contribute to the current state of the group.
4. **Dissent** - People need space to say no. Saying yes doesn't have a meaning until you are able to say no. Let people express their doubts and fears and reservations. Creating community is sloppy and messy and involves allowing people to say no.
5. **Commitment** - Commitment in a group is the promises we are willing to make to our peers. Doing great things requires commitments. Commitments in groups and accountability serve the whole. What is the price we are willing to pay for a better world?
6. **Gifts** - Rather than focusing on deficiencies in your community, focus on what people can offer. What are the unique gifts they bring to the table? Confront people with the gifts. Remember how it felt when someone saw a gift in you that you haven't recognized?

As you engage with your group, build these six conversations into the dialogue and content. Give people opportunities to dream, contribute, and take ownership.

Here is a quote from one of the members of my community of 2,400 clients and future clients called "Allebach Photography Boudoir & Couples Boudoir."

"This community has truly given me the gift of being open, without shame. It is teaching me to learn to love myself for who I am, and as I am, in every moment. I have given my heart to this group and I feel like they have accepted it and given me nothing but love in return."
- Emily Morales

Bring People Together ... In Real Life
Online communities should also give their members chances to assemble offline. It's great to get people who have never met in person but communicated online into the same room. Put together paid or free events for your small community to get together. There is a whole industry of expo companies who purely exist for the purpose of bringing people together in real life. If you've ever flown to a major city for your job to attend one of them, you know what I'm talking about. You also know how niche these conferences and expos can be.

Your tribe is looking for more ways to get involved at several different price points. Some in your group may be willing to spend thousands on flying to your event while others want a way to get involved and place their value under $100. Make places for both of these types of people to gather. These can be parties, service days, big events, or micro events. The more exclusive, the more appreciative your clients and future clients will feel.

A Quick Note about Family, Friends, Haters, and Naysayers
You've gone viral, gotten out there, and your message to the world is spreading. You are leveling up. Sadly,

not everyone is ready for you to succeed. It's easier for many people to put you in a box. Some friends or a family members just won't get it. They want comfort and predictability, and your newly elevated expert status reminds them of their dead-end job and failing business. Change is uncomfortable. Even more surprising is that some past mentors won't be able to deal with your success. If you rise above their success, expect to get thrown some shade.

Once you break the mold, once you stand out and stand up for what you believe in, you'll level up. Make no mistake. This leveling up happens on the shoulders of your haters. They will stay behind, and you'll stand on their shoulders. If you are playing big, if you believe in what you are doing, this is an expectation.

You will face critics. Your critics might be imagined, or they might be real. Author and creative Jon Acuff explains critic's math as 1 insult + 1,000 compliments = 1 insult. Be prepared for it. Realize when you are just imagining it. The ignore and unfollow button will become your friend for people who don't make the journey. Once your story spreads outside of your friendship circle, you will hit the gaggle of miserables known as the internet. They are uncouth and only wish you the worst. They are unsatisfied with their life and want to take it out on you. It's true all people have an opinion; it's just not always worth paying attention to.

Everyone has the power to create a viral personal brand capturing the attention of the media and your dream clients. It starts with showing up. It's starts with the bravery of changing our own narrative and story. We change when our story changes from what the world is doing to us to what we can do for the world. The world needs us to dream bigger because when we change our story, we change the story of the world. We are the types of people who make small movements to change our tiny slice of the world. No one has given us permission to do this. And yet here we are, believing against all odds we can make a change.

Take up the charge. You have been given the tools to spread your message. Use the tools discussed in this book. The tools for large companies use the tools we can use in our personal branding. Discover who you are at the root, what you offer; engage your dream client and their needs and the magic they get from what you offer. Believe that, if told in the right way, your story will spread, and capture the attention of your perfect clients.

As this is a book of doing, get to the work ahead of you! It's a beautiful journey. The result is always worth the sweat and tears. We'd love to hear about your journey. Join the Facebook Group "Mike Allebach's Viral Personal Branding" at http://facebook.com/groups/viralpersonalbranding to join the conversation.

Case Studies

You've heard the stories, now see pitching in action! Here are the real-world case studies. See the messages I sent to friends and the articles I've written. This is section is unedited. It's better to get things done, than things perfect. You can laugh at all of my spelling and grammar mistakes in emails and print!

Case Studies

The Local Artist

Analytics: Took video from 2 million views to 11+ million views on Facebook on George Takei Page
Result: Hundreds of inquires in the first week of promotion

Pitch to George Takei:

hello@allebachphotography... Jul 24, 2017, 8:19 AM
to teamtakei

Check it out:

I'm a wedding photographer who focuses on Tattooed Weddings. I joined up with a Lansdale ▇▇ Artist named ▇▇▇▇▇ and together we are photographing and ▇▇▇ at weddings. Our latest video has gone viral with over 2 million views.

Here is a link to the video: https://www.facebook.com/▇▇▇▇▇▇▇

- Mike Allebach
Allebach Photography

The Simple Pitch
Coverage on Daily Mail UK and Huffington Post

With people you've worked with before, 2 sentence pitches can have big results!

New Article Ideas Media Contact ×

hello@allebachphotography.com <hello@allebac... Tue, Apr 18, 2017, 3:35 PM
to ~~~~~~~~~~ bcc: mike

Are you looking to cover Couples Boudoir? Did you want me to give you an article?
-mike

Home | U.K. | News | Sports | U.S. Showbiz | Australia | Femail | Health | Science | Money | Video | Travel | Columnists | DailyMailTV
Latest Headlines | Femail | Fashion Finder | Food | Shopping | Gardening | Blogs | Parenting Blog | Games

A portrait of love: Couples of all ages and backgrounds don sexy lingerie to pose for VERY intimate boudoir shoots which 'celebrate and strengthen their relationship'

- Boudoir is a type of photography that features intimate and romantic poses
- As a way to strengthen their relationship, a group of couples have participated in their own boudoir photo shoots
- The pictures were taken by Pennsylvania-based photographer Mike Allebach, who said the photos allow 'couples to celebrate their partner'

Press Release to Cosmopolitan Magazine

Analytics: Cosmopolitan Magazine with 16 million print readers

Here is the simple press release I sent through ereleases.com which caught the eye of Cosmo

NORTH WALES, Pa., May 25, 2018 /PRNewswire/ -- Allebach Photography expanded their studio this month for the fast-growing photography niche, Couples Boudoir. This hot new trend involves people in love stripping down together for the camera.

"Couples are booking Allebach Photography to reconnect and level up their relationships. Life gets busy. People lose sight of what is important. So we focus on what they love about each other. Imagine being photographed in your underwear. It's an adventure. They laugh and have the time of their life! For many, this is relationship changing. They leave with a stronger bond than when they arrived," said Mike Allebach, Owner of Allebach Photography

Couples Boudoir is expected to triple over the next year. The experience starts with hair & makeup at the Allebach Photography studio. Then the couple gets photographed for an hour. Every couple gets to design artwork for their home or bedroom following the portrait session.

"People proudly display this wall art in their bedrooms as a reminder of their love. I can't think of a better investment into a relationship," says Mike.

About Allebach Photography

Allebach Photography opened in 2006. For 10 years the business focused on photographing tattooed brides. Allebach Photography upholds their value as an inclusive place for families of all backgrounds. Known for tattooed, LGBTQ and offbeat weddings, the company expanded into Personal Branding Headshots and Couples Boudoir in 2014. For more information, please visit http://www.allebachphotography.com

Contact
To learn more about this studio expansion and couples boudoir, contact:
Mike Allebach, Owner
403 E Walnut Street, North Wales, Pa 19454
Office: 610-539-6920

SOURCE Allebach Photography

Viral Offbeat Bride Article

Analytics: 34,000 Shares on Facebook.
Over 300,000 pageviews on Offbeat Bride
Result: Weddings booked from this article every year for 5 years.
This article was my most popular wedding booking tool.

Most wedding magazines will give you a list of questions to ask your wedding photographer: Can you describe your style? What equipment do you shoot with? Let's be real: Those questions are boring. And you probably don't actually care about the answers. So I surveyed some brides and photography-friends, and put together a list of all those questions you really want to ask, and all those things we really want you to know.

1. How do I pick a good photographer when there are hundreds listed in my area?

First, look for a forum or blog that appeals to your style. Obviously, if you're an offbeat bride, you're in the right place -- I receive my best clients through the Offbeat Bride vendor site. The photographers listed are both gay-friendly and accustomed to photographing offbeat weddings.

Narrow it down to a handful of favorites, and set up a time to meet them. Make sure you're meeting with the person who will be wielding the camera at your wedding, not a sales consultant or studio owner. You have to like, trust, and get along with your photographer -- that way you can leave the magic of photo making in the photographer's hands. Not only should you like their images, you should also like them! You'll be spending many hours with them during your wedding day.

2. How many photos do I get?

The wedding photographers I surveyed typically deliver 50-100 photos for every hour of coverage they provide. Four hundred photos may seem like a lot, but your wedding photographer is preserving all those little details and the moments you missed while you were mingling.

3. I love those photos with the blurry backgrounds. How do you get that look?
You're talking about bokeh -- a Japanese word roughly translated as "fuzzy." Photographers get that look by using professional lenses that separate the subject from the background.

4. I found one photographer whose images look soft and pastel, one whose images look clean, and one whose images look like they were shot on old film. What's the deal?

Every photographer has a different way of editing their images using computer software (the high-tech version of a darkroom). This is called "Post-Processing." Most photographers do some basic lighting and color adjustments, but you can also use editing software to create a unique look. Three popular styles right now are:

Clean - lightly processed to appear natural

Matte - a low-contrast look with muted colors, similar to vintage film

High Contrast - a vibrant look with rich colors that pop

It doesn't matter which style you go with, as long as you love it!

5. Why is wedding photography so freakin' expensive?

This is the question I see most from brides on the interwebs. Wedding photography seems like easy money -- work for one day and rake in the cash, right? But most full-time wedding photographers I know carry over $15,000 worth of wedding gear and often work 60-hour weeks. (Remember those 800 images from question #2? It takes several full days just to edit those.) Add insurance, taxes, software, advertising, albums, repair, shipping, and studio expenses, and many photographers end up making less than minimum wage for the first few years of their career.

6. How can I make sure I look good in my photos?

Relax. If you're relaxed, it'll come through in your photos. Leave some breathing room in your schedule so you don't feel rushed -- I recommend a minimum 30 minutes for family and wedding party photos, and an hour for the bride and groom. Oh, and get plenty of sleep and drink lots of water the night before. Take it easy at the rehearsal dinner. Wedding-day hangovers are not fun.

7. I keep hearing about "shoot and burn" photography. Sounds painful. What is it?

Actually, yeah, it can be kind of painful. "Shoot and burn" is slang for photographing a wedding and burning it straight to CD without post-processing. It's usually super cheap -- for a reason. Bad lighting isn't corrected, distracting elements aren't removed (hello, Speedo-clad photobomber!), and zits remain proudly on display. You're left with the kind of photos that end up on Buzzfeed's fail feed.

Digital files may be important to you, but find a full-service photographer who will edit the images and print reference proofs before handing over the digis. And please, don't let the digitals rot on your hard drive. As a photographer, I want you to proudly display your wedding photos. It makes me sad when I think of all the photos that never get printed. Don't hide your wedding photos! I tell my clients to hang up a large print or two -- when you're having a crappy day, it's great to look up in your living room and see a photo of an awesome day.

8. Should we do a "first look"? And, um, what the hell is a "first look"?

The first look is a chance for wedding couples to see each other privately before the ceremony. Two-thirds of my clients currently opt to do a first look. It's a great chance to get the wedding jitters out and spend a few minutes alone together. I find that first look photos tend to be some of my favorites. It's a real moment with real emotions. Honestly, it's also a great way to avoid stress on your wedding day. (Some of my couples even choose to get ready together!) And many of my couples get to enjoy their whole cocktail hour because they got all of the photos out of the way before the wedding.

9. Do I really need a second photographer?

No one needs a second photographer, but they can provide you with more images and a different perspective. Many of the top photographers only work with assistants who carry gear and help with professional lighting. The best thing is to ask your wedding photographer to see how they prefer to work. You can get good results either way.

10. How far in advance should I book a wedding photographer?

Many in-demand wedding photographers book weddings at over a year out. As it gets closer to your wedding date, it will be harder to book your first-choice photographer. If your favorite photographer is unavailable on your date, don't panic. Ask them for recommendations -- they may know someone with a similar style and a lighter schedule.

11. You can Photoshop that, right?

It depends. As I photographer, I want to get everything is perfect as possible in camera. Posing, location scouting, and camera settings can "fix" most things before I even click the shutter. If your uncle photobombs you, I'm going to retake the photo -- it's much easier to get the photo right than to fix it with Photoshop. Many photographers charge for extensive editing in Photoshop, because it can be very time consuming.

12. Should I tip my photographer?

I get asked this a lot. There was a great article about tipping on Offbeat Bride. For photographers, "Tips are never expected but are always appreciated."

Hopefully this clears up some burning questions about wedding photography -- and makes it a little bit easier to find the perfect photographer for your wedding day. Let me know what you think!

Offbeat Bride Guest post written by Mike Allebach
Mike Allebach (aka The Tattooed Bride Photographer) is a wedding photographer who also writes tips for tattooed brides, and has an unhealthy addiction to Taco Tuesday.

See more work at allebachphotography.com

The Twitter to TV

 Mike "couples boudoir" Allebach @michaelallebach · 4 Jun 2018
This is the most insane wedding photo ever taken by my friend Ashley Fisher a Photographer from St. Louis over the weekend.

photo: Ashley Fisher

 Ray Prop checked in to 📍 Fox2Now.
25 mins · St. Louis, MO

I was interviewed by Lisa Hart this morning. Thank you Momo for always being by my side. Shout out to Ashley Fisher Photography, we wish you were here with us.

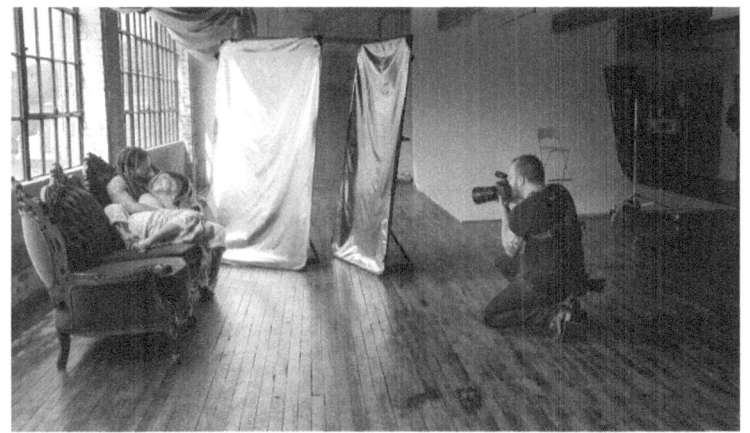
photo: Annie Vickrey

Connect to Your Badass

Everyone deserves a photography experience to explore who they are and the people they love. Mike Allebach uses photography to connect you to your badass. Visit allebachphotography.com to schedule your session at his Philadelphia suburbs studio whether you want headshots, personal branding photos or couples boudoir. Don't wait another day. Your best life awaits.

Book photography, podcasts, speaking engagements via hello@allebachphotography.com or call 610.539.6920

Join the conversation
Ask questions and tell us about your successes! Continue the discussion and get the worksheets on Facebook at
Mike Allebach's Viral Personal Branding
https://www.facebook.com/groups/viralpersonalbranding/

www.ingramcontent.com/pod-product-compliance
Lightning Source LLC
Chambersburg PA
CBHW030653220526
45463CB00005B/1756